Daily Choices for Christ

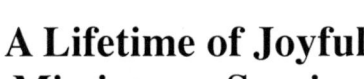

A Lifetime of Joyful
Missionary Service

by

Helen Jean Moose Zwyghuizen

Philippians 4:13

Copyright © 2007 by Helen Jean Moose Zwyghuizen

Daily Choices for Christ
by Helen Jean Moose Zwyghuizen

Printed in the United States of America

ISBN 978-1-60034-943-0
ISBN 1-60034-943-9

All rights reserved solely by the author. The author guarantees all contents are original and do not infringe upon the legal rights of any other person or work. No part of this book may be reproduced in any form without the permission of the author. The views expressed in this book are not necessarily those of the publisher.

Unless otherwise indicated, Bible quotations are taken from the King James Version of the Bible.

www.xulonpress.com

Table of Contents

Chapter 1 - Transfusion..9

Chapter 2 - She Became A Christian...15

Chapter 3 - The Choice is Yours — Victory or Defeat! 19

Chapter 4 - Baptism...21

Chapter 5 - The Lord Leads...25

Chapter 6 - God Calls..31

Chapter 7 - What Next?...33

Chapter 8 - Bible School...37

Chapter 9 - Bible School - continued.................................41

Chapter 10 - Teaching Again...45

Chapter 11 - Flying School..49

Chapter 12 - God's Protection 53

Chapter 13 - The Home Office..57

Chapter 14 - Deputation 61

Chapter 15 - Waiting..65

Chapter 16 - On Board Ship 67

Chapter 17 - Landing...71

Chapter 18 - China at Last! 75

Chapter 19 - On The Move For The Lord 79

Chapter 20 - War on the Way 83

Chapter 21 - Noso Chief 87

Chapter 22 - War in Chengdu – 1949...93

Chapter 23 - Food in China 1950..97

Chapter 24 - Uncertain Days in 1950 101

Chapter 25 - Student Work 1950 105

Chapter 26 - The Move Is On 109

Chapter 27 - Last Days in China 113

Chapter 28 - Leaving China..119

Chapter 29 - Give Up Being a Missionary? No!........................125

Chapter 30 - Off To Indonesia 129

Chapter 31 - Struggles Faced In Indonesia 135

Chapter 32 - The Lord Increases The Sunday School.............141

Chapter 33 - Result of Visitation 149

Chapter 34 - Young People's Choir 153

Chapter 35 - Yearly Camping 161

Chapter 36 - Home On Furlough 165

Chapter 37 - Be Of Good Courage 169

Chapter 38 - Alone On The Station 175

Chapter 39 - Making Room For More Members 179

Chapter 40 - Anything Could Happen 183

Chapter 41 - The Ultimatum – Go Home Or Get Married!...187

God Gives Credit To Those Deserving It 193

Chapter 1
Transfusion

God was at work early in Helen Jean Moose's life to teach her many lessons. During the great depression her family all learned to work to help it to exist. Life could be hard in southern Minnesota. Often she worked for their neighbors. She liked Mrs. Drummond and helped her many times.

One day a neighbor, Mrs. Drummond, fell sick. She needed a blood transfusion before she could have an operation or she would die.

Her husband and sons were healthy so they expected to give her blood. Their blood, however, was not the right type to match Mrs. Drummond's. She had O-RH negative blood. They all had positive blood. They advertised they would pay money to anyone who was willing to give blood if they had O-RH negative blood type.

In those days there was no such thing as a blood bank. In fact, even blood transfusions were uncommon. Days went by and Mrs. Drummond was getting weaker and weaker. Still no one was found with O-RH negative blood.

One day after school, Helen Jean started to think. What if she died? What kind of blood did she herself have? The only way to find out was to go see her 4-H Club doctor. Ask him, he could tell her. She had no idea that he was Mrs. Drummond's doctor. Soon she was in for a big surprise.

He was glad to see she was willing to find out about her own blood. In no time he had a slide with a drop of Mrs. Drummond's blood on it and a drop of Helen Jean's on it. The two mixed. Helen Jean had O-RH negative blood.

Out of many, many people, she was the first to match Mrs. Drummond's. Helen could give blood if her parents would let her.

The doctor advised her to go home and tell her parents that out of many, many people she was the only one who could help Mrs. Drummond. The doctor would like her, if possible, to give blood that week.

Helen Jean went home and told her parents that the doctor had found a donor for Mrs. Drummond. But when they found out it was their daughter their attitude changed. Mother scolded, father was sure his daughter would die.

The parents, Raymond & Myrtle Moose

The doctor calmed their nerves. Helen Jean would go to school and get permission from the principal to leave school about 10 o'clock, go to the hospital, give blood and return about 2 o'clock. The principal gave permission and at the appointed time Helen Jean walked alone to the hospital.

She was taken to a hospital room, given orders to undress and put on a gown. Shortly after this, the nurses came with a stretcher. Helen Jean hopped aboard and was rolled into the operating room.

When she arrived she saw a small table with a little machine with two lengths of rubber tubing. Each one had piece of glass tubing in it. At one end of each rubber tube was a needle.

Very shortly in came another stretcher. Mrs. Drummond had arrived. Wah! How thin and pale she looked. There was no color in her face.

The doctor put a tourniquet on Helen Jean's arm and inserted the needle at the end of the rubber tubing into a big fat vein of Helen's arm. That being done, he went to Mrs. Drummond. What a picnic the doctor had to find a vein in Mrs. Drummond's arm. Her veins were so small. After a long period of time of hunting for a vein, one was found.

All was ready. The doctor sat on a stool near the machine and started to turn a crank. Blood started to come from Helen Jean's arm through the glass of the rubber tubing to the machine. From the machine it went through the rubber tubing to Mrs. Drummond's arm. You could see it move in the glass tubing on her side.

The doctor cranked and cranked. Suddenly the machine stopped. Helen Jean could give no more blood. She had given 80 cc or about one half cup of blood to Mrs. Drummond.

Wah! Helen Jean looked over at Mrs. Drummond. She looked a bit pink. The doctor was pleased. He had hoped to get a pint of blood but Helen Jean could not give that much. Her blood was young and free of disease so it would immediately help Mrs. Drummond.

Helen Jean was rolled back to her room and told to try to take a nap. When she awoke, she saw a big dinner tray awaiting her. After dinner she was told she could go back to school.

Mrs. Drummond soon had her operation and was back home with Moose blood in her veins and feeling good again. She lived several years after that operation. The blood had extended her life. Without the right kind of blood she would have died that year.

After Helen Jean became a Christian she thought about Jesus giving His blood for her.

1. She gave for one of her friends.
    1. Jesus gave for enemies as well as friends.

2. She walked alone to the hospital to give blood.
    2. Jesus walked with enemies as well as friends to the cross.

3. She was given a gown.
    3. Jesus had His clothes taken from Him.

4. People were proud of a teenager giving blood to a friend.
    4. They made fun of Jesus.

5. When she gave blood they used a machine.
    5. When Jesus gave blood they used nails and a spear.

6. She had O-RH Negative blood which was only useful for a few people.
    6. The blood of Jesus fits all who will believe He died for them.

7. Her father was not happy she gave blood.
    7. God the Father was proud that Jesus gave His blood.

8. She gave only 80 cc's of blood.
    8. Jesus gave all of His blood. He died.

9. She helped Mrs. Drummond live for a few more years.
    9. The blood of Jesus enables one to live forever.

10. Her blood was human blood.
   10. The blood of Jesus has power to forgive sin for it was God's own blood.

11. When she gave her blood nothing unusual happened.
   11. When Jesus died there was darkness. The Temple veil was rent.

12. She was given money for her blood.
   12. The blood of Jesus paid for sinners' home in Heaven.

13. She gave up a half a day of school to give blood.
   13. Jesus gave His life.

14. She went back to school after giving blood.
   14. Jesus died. He was buried but arose from the grave for He was God.

15. God used Helen Jean's blood to help one lady, Mrs. Drummond, to have physical life.
   15. God used the blood of Jesus Christ His Son to help anyone who would believe in Him have eternal life.

Chapter 2
She Became A Christian

The news came out in the newspapers that the world was coming to the end the next day. This took place while Helen Jean was in grade school.

Esther, a sister of Helen Jean, a friend, Myrtle Nelson, and Helen Jean were playing ball on the Sunday before this took place. They discussed the issue. Helen Jean was fearful and wished she really knew how to become a Christian. Her family did not go to church at that time, so she knew of no one to ask about the situation.

How glad she was the next day when the news was only a rumor!

Not long after that Helen Jean's mother decided the children should be in Sunday school.

Sunday morning came and they went to Wheaton, Minnesota, to the Presbyterian Church. They were having their last Sunday school class that day until the next fall. Next week they would have no Sunday school.

The teacher took Esther and Helen Jean to class. She had not expected to teach so she asked them if they knew John 3:16. They had not heard of it. The whole class was spent in learning the verse. "What a long verse," they thought. Esther managed to say it but Helen Jean could not say it perfectly.

For Christmas Mother decided to give each of the girls a Bible. They were so glad for them. They started to read them. They started in Genesis. When Esther arrived in Leviticus, she stopped. Helen

Jean continued on but it was difficult. After some time she too gave up reading the Bible.

The folks moved to Alexandria, Minnesota. Helen Jean was in the sixth grade. She had a friend who invited her to the Methodist release-time class from school one day a week.

This led to her going to Sunday school there. Helen Jean asked her Sunday school teacher how to become a Christian. She said, "Believe on the Lord Jesus Christ". Well, she believed there was a Jesus; that He was God; that He died on the cross; that He arose again. But she knew she was not a Christian. She was a sinner no one needed to tell her. She knew she was. All through high school when she would have a new Sunday school teacher, she would ask them the same question. She would get the same answer.

Grandma Moose

After graduating from high school she was enrolled in the Normal Training School for Teachers in Alexandria, Minnesota. However, Grandma Moose needed someone to run her rooming house and father needed a job so they moved to Montevideo, Minnesota, to help her. Helen Jean transferred to the Normal Training School in Montevideo.

That summer mother found Esther and Helen Jean a job of selling dance tickets with a gambling device of five cars on them. The Veterans of Foreign Wars put out these tickets. The best place to sell these tickets was in beer joints or taverns. On Sunday a good place to sell them was in front of a church that believed in lottery.

More and more Helen Jean wanted to become a Christian. But how?

One Sunday morning she decided to go up the street and see if she could find a church in Montevideo which could help her.

At the top of the hill was a church without paint, a sign needing repair, and long grass in the lawn. That church had no appeal to her. She looked on down the street and saw a good-sized Methodist Church. The lawn was trimmed and looked inviting.

She pushed open the heavy door a crack and saw a number of young people her age sitting in the auditorium. The young people's Sunday school teacher had not yet arrived for some reason, and the young people were put with the adults. How the Lord led. She quickly and quietly sat down to listen.

She sat with a nice person, whose fingernails and lips were not red like her own. She must be a Christian, Helen Jean thought.

She listened and too soon the lesson was over.

The young people noticed her and came around to greet her. They invited her to come to young people's meeting that evening. This was great so she went.

October 4 came and the young people in a group decided to go to a camp on the edge of town. Two of the young people invited her to go with them. She could not refuse.

The three of them sat near the front while the rest sat in a group in a long back row. They determined to pray for Helen Jean that she would become a Christian that night.

Helen Jean did not remember what the camp speaker spoke about, but when he gave the invitation he said, "If anyone would like to become a Christian come down to the front."

If he would have given any other kind of invitation she would not have understood.

He evidently, Helen Jean thought, must know how to become a Christian so she got up from her bench and started to the front. All of a sudden she thought, am I the only one doing this? Then she said to herself, "It doesn't matter; tonight I want to become a Christian." She arrived at the front where the speaker was standing and in a gruff tone said, "Kneel down." She did.

There was no floor in the camp and they had put hay on the ground this year rather than sawdust. She kneeled down but that didn't make her a Christian. There she was in the hay. Nothing happened, for coming to the front of a camp meeting does not make you a Christian.

They were singing "Softly and Tenderly, Jesus is Calling": but even that song did not make her a Christian.

Finally, in desperation while kneeling there in the hay, she cried out "Oh, Lord, I want to be a Christian tonight, but I don't know how."

With lightning speed she thought of Acts 16:31 which she had learned in Sunday school. "And they said, 'Believe on the Lord Jesus Christ and thou shalt be saved and thy house.'"

"But Lord, she prayed, "I believe Jesus died on the cross; I believe He was buried; I believe He arose from the dead; I believe He is God, but I am not a Christian."

Instantly she realized He died for <u>her sin</u>. Wah! The tears came. He died for <u>all her sin.</u> How good He was to her.

The young people in the back row were all praying. At that moment they looked up and one after another said I believe she is a Christian. Their prayers were answered. Helen Jean had a new relationship with the Lord Jesus Christ. This new relationship would change her whole life and it did. This was Helen Jean's new birthday, October 4, 1936.

God used the Scripture she had learned after going to Sunday school to help her be saved and to grow spiritually.

Chapter 3
The Choice is Yours – Victory or Defeat!

No one needed to tell Helen Jean that she was a sinner. Daily she knew she was. While in high school her gym teacher taught her to tap-dance. She loved it. Often she was found turning on the radio to the jazziest song she could find then she would tap out her latest step. While setting the table often she would practice tap dancing around the table.

Her dream was to go to Hollywood some day to be a dancer, but God had other plans for her.

After she became a Christian she realized her music and her dancing were not pleasing to the Lord, so in her own strength she tried to eliminate both.

When she became a Christian October 4, 1936 she was enrolled in the Montevideo Teacher's Training School. Shortly after this, the normal school training teacher decided the girls in the school should go to the park to see the lovely colors, to have a wiener roast, and to get to know one another.

After roasting wieners and eating to the full, the girls suggested Helen Jean tap dance for them. She refused. The whole crowd with one voice demanded she tap. She made the excuse there was no suitable place in the park to tap. One of the girls said she would clear the picnic table and she could tap there. Oh no, how could she! However, peer pressure helped push her into tapping on top of the picnic table. When she climbed off the picnic table she was a defeated Christian in spite of all the compliments she received. That night she told the

Lord that was the last time she would tap. That was the end of her tap dancing. How gracious the Lord was to forgive her. He also took the desire to go to Hollywood away from her.

Dancing from that day on was not a problem but the jazz music still plagued her.

The radio did not seem to play Christian music. One song that came to mind often was "Tomatoes are cheaper, potatoes are cheaper, now's the time to fall in love." Too often this song would come to mind and she would be singing it before she realized it.

She didn't remember when she first heard the chorus "I Walk with the King, Hallelujah", but she started to sing this when worldly songs started to haunt her. The louder she sang the sooner the song left her. This chorus became a real life saver in overcoming worldly songs whenever they plagued her.

Helen Jean learned peer pressure is very strong but the Lord Jesus can help you overcome. She also learned the Lord works in many ways if you will trust Him to help you when you want to be used by Him. She found to say "yes" to people's desire for her was far easier than to say "no". However, now that she was a Christian, just what did the Lord want her to say and do?

Chapter 4
Baptism

Daily Helen Jean read her Bible. She found many ways in which her life should be more Christlike.

Her mother had an interdenominational church background and her father a Methodist background. However, he did not believe in babies being baptized. As a result none of the children were baptized as babies.

Helen Jean could not find in the Bible where babies were baptized so she agreed with her father. Nevertheless, she wanted to be baptized now that she had become a Christian.

She found in Acts 8 about the Ethiopian who went down into the water and was baptized. Jesus was baptized in a river. She could not see how a few sprinkles of water could be called baptism. With this mind set she did not want to join the local Methodist Church who sprinkled.

She talked to some of the young people about baptism and found they too had not been baptized either. That was a surprise to her.

After being graduated from Montevideo Teacher's Training School Helen Jean for the summer took a job as a housemaid caring for four children while their mother worked in her husband's business. Arrangements were made so Helen Jean could have one week off for camp.

Dr. Reese was the senior pastor of First Covenant Church of Minneapolis. Each year he and his church held camp at Medicine Lake. The camp had been built by men from the Minneapolis City

Mission. A stone cutter had been saved and he cut many of the stones for the main buildings. The camp was beautiful. Some of the other workers of the City Mission had made pews using birch logs. The smaller white birch logs were used to frame the back of the pews giving the chapel a clean appearance.

The cabins for the campers were made in the form of a tepee. One large dorm had three stories which was like a wigwam. Helen Jean and the Montevideo girls stayed in one of the rooms on the third floor.

Wigwam camp dorm where the girls stayed

One day the leaders of the camp announced that there was going to be a baptismal service. It would be held in the lake. Helen Jean and a number of the group from Montevideo went to the leaders to see if they could be included in the group that would be baptized. The leaders were pleased that these from Montevideo who had not been baptized wanted to be baptized.

After the leaders of the Covenant Church were sure of each of their faith in the Lord Jesus Christ they were willing to baptize them on the condition that they join their local church. Minneapolis Covenant Church could not care for them for they were about three hundred miles away. They wanted the young people to attend a good church where the Bible was preached. This was not a problem with the young people. They would join the Methodist Church when they got home.

The day of baptism arrived. The sun was out. The day was a wonderful summer day. About twenty people went down into the water one by one including Helen Jean. What a happy bunch.

After the evening meal and service the young people met at the empty pop stand. They sat around and sang as one of them started choruses to sing. At the end of the week no one wanted to go home. However, camp was over so they piled into the bus to go back to Montevideo.

The next time the invitation was given to join the church the whole gang responded. The pastor was disappointed he had not had the privilege of sprinkling them, but was glad they were coming into the church. They were a help to the church in many ways. They sang in choir, taught Sunday school and helped wherever they could.

Mrs. Elkjer still greatly encouraged them spiritually in all the ways she could. What a blessing she was to them all!

Chapter 5
The Lord Leads

The young people of the Methodist Church took a great interest in helping Helen Jean grow spiritually.

Orda Munster invited her to drop in anytime. Orda loved to play the piano and sing. Helen Jean would sit on the piano bench with her and sing hymns. What good times they had together! She learned many hymns this way.

Charles Elkjer, a strong Christian young man, was attending a junior college. He was about Helen Jean's age. They started dating. His mother was a wonderful Christian and invited the young people to come to their house for prayer meeting and Christian help. They called this meeting the "Inner Circle". There was no set time for Inner Circle. Word was passed around and off they went to the Elkjer home.

Charles' father was not a Christian but was not at home much. He was the town's banker.

Charles gave Helen Jean a book with many helpful suggestions for a new Christian. He loved to walk her home after meetings to hear her reaction of what took place. As they prayed together Helen Jean grew spiritually.

The day came when Charles told Helen Jean he was going to Asbury College next year. Oh, how she wished she could go too.

She told her folks she would like to go to Asbury. They thought otherwise.

Dad told her she was going to teach school. She had gone to normal school, and many schools were begging for teachers. The county superintendent gave them some names of school board members near there that needed teachers.

In tears, Helen Jean got dressed to meet men on the school boards. Father took her to see them, told her to dry her tears, and be businesslike. The first school evidently had already found a teacher. "Good", thought Helen Jean. This did not discourage father. On and on they went until at last they found a school that hired her for $60 a month. This was good wages for some teachers were only getting $40 a month.

The first year Helen Jean's sister, Esther, picked her up Friday nights and they would go home to Montevideo. There Helen Jean met the old crowd, went to church and often went to the hospital to sing for an outreach of the young people. Mrs. Elkjer encouraged Helen Jean to read her Bible and pray.

The Moose elementary school bus

The sad day arrived when Mr. Elkjer, the banker, was promoted to another town and Charles went off to Asbury College. Esther changed schools so did not pick her up anymore.

Daily Choices for Christ

In the spring when contracts must be signed Helen Jean decided to apply to a school on the highway between Clara City and Montevideo. She was able to get a boarding place nearby. She walked to and from school. She asked about a good church in the area.

There was a Baptist Church in Maynard, Minnesota. The pastor lived on the highway a few miles from her boarding place. The first Sunday Zola, the daughter of the people where she boarded, took her. Zola was not interested in this church for she was a Christian Scientist, but she would introduce her to the church.

When the pastor found out where she was boarding he told her he would pick her up anytime she wanted to go. Wah! She wanted to go anytime the doors were open.

Kenneth Nelson, the young pastor was helping his mother since his father had died. His folks had a cattle farm. What a blessing and help spiritually he was to Helen Jean. She told him of her dream when she was twenty-one that she wanted to go to Asbury College. He suggested Northwestern Bible School, which was in Minneapolis, Minnesota not so far away. She could work half days and go to school half days.

At the end of that happy year she signed the contract for another year to teach not knowing things would really change. When she heard Kenneth was getting married and had a church in Ohio, her heart sank. How would she get to church? Why didn't he tell her he was going to marry his close friend from Northwestern Bible School?

The new pastor lived in town so there was no way Helen Jean could get to church.

Helen Jean had driven a tractor but not a car. She was stuck in the country with no bus to Maynard to go to church. The only way was to buy a second hand car and drive herself.

She wrote to the second hand car business in Montevideo and asked them to bring out a good second hand car that she could buy. She would have to use some of her hard-earned money saved for school and then sell it before she went off to school.

The dealer came out to the school in his own car and told her she could come with him and pick out one for herself. She prayed

"Lord, give me a good car, one I can use to go to church". Together they looked over the cars in the lot. How she prayed the Lord would direct her to the right one. The first one they tried was nice but the motor didn't seem to sound right to her. She asked if there was another. There was but it would need seat covers. They hopped in and she watched him drive. It sounded like it should. It was not a fancy one, only a Model A Ford needing seat covers, but the paint and motor were in good shape. It would get her to church and back. She said, "I will take it".

After they made a contract, for she would pay for it in a few months, she asked him to teach her to drive. He was shocked. She had picked out the best second hand car in the lot and didn't know how to drive but the Lord did the picking for her. That night the Lord enabled her to drive to the prayer meeting in Maynard.

In those days you did not need to have a car drivers' license to drive, but after a few weeks Helen Jean got her first Minnesota drivers' license.

The new pastor was Rev. Harvey Hill. He and his wife with three children were a great help to Helen Jean.

They found out that Helen Jean was having doubts about her salvation. They invited her to come to the parsonage for a snack. Over the snack Mrs. Hill asked, "Helen Jean, when does everlasting life end"?

The only answer Helen Jean could think of was "when you sin!"

Mrs. Hill said, "Then it's not everlasting life is it"?

Mrs. Hill went on to explain, "Once you have everlasting life it never ends" using Scripture.

Helen Jean shook her head, "That can't be true." Mrs. Hill gave her verses from the Bible, but Helen Jean decided it was time for her to leave and she did. When she got to her boarding place she went to her room. She could not dismiss from her thoughts the verses that Mrs. Hill had given her. She got down on her knees and praised God she was really a Christian whether she felt like it or not at times. Again joy filled her being.

Pastor Hill and his wife had both gone to Northwestern Bible School. The more Helen Jean thought about Bible school training the more she thought this was the school for her. If the folks wanted to see her they could, for they went to Minneapolis now and then. She could work and pay for her board and room. As for the money she had saved, it would go for tuition.

Helen Jean the teacher (right front)
with sister Esther, Dad, and 2 brothers

Chapter 6
God Calls

After Pastor Harvey Hill became the minister in the Maynard Baptist Church, he saw the need of the church reaching out to the lost around the world. He invited some SIM missionaries to come. Mr. Harold Street came and presented a real challenge. Helen Jean realized she could do work in Africa but somehow she questioned this, did the Lord want her to go to Africa or China? She thought it would be far easier to go to Africa.

The next day at school the thoughts came and went, go to Africa, after Bible school.

Each night after teaching she would sit and have devotions before she went back to her boarding place for there was no time to be quiet and pray before she went to bed. The light in her room was poor so the best place for devotions was at school in her empty classroom.

She had to know. Where does the Lord want me to go — Africa or China? The missionary had made Africa so appealing. She realized that would be nice for her. But was it God's will?

She prayed and after sometime she asked the Lord to show her if she should go to China or not. She knew the word "China" was not in the Bible. She was desperate. She was torn to go to Africa yet was that what the Lord wanted?

She took her Bible and asked the Lord to show her from the Bible what to do after Bible school. She opened the Bible and read II Timothy 1:15 "This thou knowest that all they which are in Asia be turned away from me;". "Asia" seemed to jump out to her. After that Africa was never a problem to her. She knew God wanted her in the Orient.

A few years later when Helen Jean appeared before the mission to become a missionary she found they had no work in the Orient.

They asked her if she would consider going to Africa. She immediately said, "God has not called me to Africa and if I can not go under this mission to China I must find another.

They dismissed her. She wondered now what? However, she was at peace whatever the Lord wanted she wanted.

Later in the day, to her surprise, the mission announced that she was accepted for China. She would leave as soon as another missionary was accepted and they both had their support.

Little did she know what a rocky road was ahead but she was at peace for if God wanted her in China He would enable her to endure whatever would take place and He did.

Chapter 7
What Next?

Rev. Fleming, an American Sunday School Union missionary, was the father of Roseline Fleming who taught in Maynard Public Schools. She attended the Maynard Baptist Church. Helen Jean and Roseline became good friends and both wanted to please the Lord.

Rev. Fleming needed teachers to help teach Daily Vacation Bible School as soon as the public schools were out.

Along with a number of others, Roseline and Helen Jean found their way to the week of instruction for the summer's work of teaching Daily Vacation Bible School in that area. Each of the young people stayed in homes opened to them for the week.

The first night before Helen Jean retired, the head of the house invited her to come and have family devotions with them. He read a portion of Scripture and then said a few words. This was new to Helen Jean. What a blessing! After his remarks about the Scripture each of the family prayed. This was too much for Helen Jean. She had become comfortable teaching public school. She knew God wanted her in China, but she also knew what a struggle it would be to go to Bible school. That night she realized she was twenty-one. She also knew that her folks thought differently and the pull to do her folks' will would be far easier than to go against them and be a missionary. However, that night in tears she decided to go to Bible school at Northwestern Bible School that fall. The next step after teaching Daily Vacation Bible School for the summer was to tell her parents she was finished teaching public school. She had to go to Bible school!

The DVBS conference where Helen Jean was called to missions

After a blessed summer of teaching several one-week Bible schools, Helen Jean went home. Her folks had moved from Montevideo, Minnesota, to Donaldson, Minnesota, in the northwestern part of the state.

The farm her father had obtained had no buildings so the family had rented a house in Donaldson.

Across the road from the Moose farm was another farm for sale with several buildings. Helen Jean's dad wanted to buy it but his credit had not been established. No one would lend him a down payment. Even his mother or brothers did not think much of such an investment. There was only one hope. Maybe his two-schoolteacher daughters would help him.

Esther had just bought a new car. Payments were due each month so she was not able to help her father obtain a farm home.

Helen Jean had saved money and sold her car for Bible school tuition, which she hoped would be enough for three years. After some thought and prayer, Helen Jean suggested her Dad could use her school money if he would pay back enough for tuition each year until it was paid. She did not expect interest, only what she lent to him. The down payment was made and the farmhouse was made ready for the Moose family.

Helen Jean would not let herself think, "What if this was Satan's way of keeping her out of Bible school?" However, the Scripture says, "Honor thy father and mother...". This was one way she could do this.

The day came when she must leave to go to Bible school. Mother fussed and cried. Dad said she was throwing her life away going to Bible school. He wanted her to make money and be someone.

She was accepted at Northwestern Bible School for the fall. The folks had hoped she would change her mind by September, but she had to follow the Lord's leading.

Helen Jean's Dad made it very plain that he and her mother had no money to pay for her schooling. She would have to work. At Northwestern, however, there was a good employment office. Many of the students worked half days.

The money she prayed she had loaned would giver her enough for her tuition. She would not be able to stay in a dorm, but work for her board and room. She did one better. She got a job as a maid with board, room and $3.00 a week besides!

When time came to leave for school, Helen Jean's Dad would not let her take a bus to Minneapolis, but drove her to the school. He wanted to see what kind of situation his daughter would have.

He was a bit impressed by the school, which had a good employment office. After registration they went there. Mrs. Wilcox was very kind and told her that there was a good job awaiting her in the Lake Harriet area.

She and her dad went there and found Mrs. Wilcox's word was true. Both were impressed at the work. Right behind the house was the Lake Harriet Baptist Church. She could attend services there and not have to spend carfare to go to church.

In the first year of Bible school each student must sing in a church choir. There were five young people going to Northwestern who attended this church. All were first year students. What a blessed time they had together.

The Lord had prepared this wonderful spot to challenge Helen Jean's Dad.

Chapter 8
Bible School

What a privilege the Lord had given to Helen Jean to go to Bible school half days and work half days. However, she found that many of the students were at least four or five years younger than she was. Her thinking was the mission field after finishing Bible school. Most of the students had no aim in going to Bible school. Many of them were helped and stayed in the dorm. Nevertheless she found the students who went to Lake Harriet Baptist Church were older and had a burden for the Lord's work. This was a comfort to her.

While she was in Montevideo Charles Elkjer had given her a little leather New Testament. She treasured it and carried it in her purse. The day came when she heard from Charles. He felt God was calling him to South America. Wah! She felt she was called to China.

Her second cousin had gone to China and had come home during the Boxer Rebellion. She married a Post Office man and never went back. As a result her life had not been a happy one.

No, she could not go to South America. God had called her to China. She wrapped up her treasured New Testament and sent it off to Charles, but not without a flood of tears. She dearly missed that New Testament, but had a peace about what she had done. It was what the Lord wanted her to do.

Minneapolis is noted for flu during the winter months. The day came when Helen Jean got the flu. She was quite sick but she had to go to school. Each day she missed caused too much make-up work. It became hard to study so her grades went down.

To make matters worse, the lady of the house who worked down town was laid off. She told Helen Jean she was fired too, but she could stay there until she found a job.

Wah! Did the Lord really want her in Bible school? She wrote her folks telling them all her troubles. One week later a letter came from her mother, encouraging her to come home. They would find her a school to teach.

Praise the Lord, the letter took a week to arrive and during that time Helen Jean found another job near there. She felt much better, and was determined to get better grades. Helen Jean looked back on this event many times in her life to praise the Lord the letter took so long in coming and that she did not give up going to Bible school.

The first year of Bible school was about to end when Esther Rinner came to Helen Jean and asked her to go with her to Montana for the summer. The Bible school had been invited by the missionaries out there to teach Bible school and help in camps. They would have to pay their own way coming and going. Helen had saved some to go home which was about half way there. Could she save enough to get there and back? That was a good question. The more she prayed about this the more she knew it was the Lord's will to go. Rose Voetman heard about this and also decided to go. Not long after this Esther was not able to go.

Rose and Helen started out taking the train part way and the bus the rest of the way. On the train they saw a little deaf and dumb girl. They wrote on a paper saying they wanted her to teach them how to give the gospel by signing. She was happy to do that. Rose and Helen Jean worked hard to learn enough to give the gospel on their fingers. Moorhead, Minnesota, came all too soon. They had to get off the train to catch the bus. While on the bus they practiced their new method of giving the gospel. The bus driver noticed them and asked them what they were saying on their fingers. He had a friend in a few stops from there who could prove whether they truly were talking with their hands.

At the appointed stop the bus driver got off and immediately came back with a man and told the girls to go to work with their hands. They did and he understood. After they gave him the gospel, all that they had learned, he wanted to talk with them. However, they told him this was all they had time to learn. The bus driver was ready to go so the man went back to the station. The girls praised the Lord that they had learned at least enough to give him the gospel.

Rose and Helen Jean spent a delightful summer filled with many experiences in Daily Vacation Bible Schools and camp in that lovely scenic state. They left to go home, praising God for the privilege of giving the gospel to needy people.

When Helen Jean arrived home she realized her father was having a problem. The war was taking all available men for services. There were very few men to help on the farms. Helen Jean's dad had hired an old man, Mr. Tweedie, to come and work as a tractor man. There was no one for the combine. Mr. Tweedie was a Christian and taught the adult Sunday school class in the Lutheran Church. Helen Jean had no fear of working with him so she became his combine manager. He was very careful to miss the potholes, which were the wet spots and slowed down if the grain was piled too high for the feeder to take the grain. As a result of his carefulness they accomplished a great deal of work without breaking down or plugging up the combine.

September came and again Helen Jean headed off to Bible school. Her mother saw to it that she had enough money for her tuition from that which she loaned her father. How she praised the Lord she could go to Bible school with a much better attitude from the home folks. A job awaited her as soon as she arrived in Minneapolis.

Chapter 9
Bible School Continued

During her first year in Bible School Helen Jean had signed up to sing in the choir for the radio. They practiced during school hours and sang on the air three times each week. She enjoyed this ministry very much, but sometimes the director would have special practices on Thursdays when she wanted to go to prayer meeting. This was a hardship for her for she had to take a street car to the school downtown and then return home alone on the street car. Prayer meeting was more important to her. In her second year, in spite of enjoying singing on the radio, she gave it up for prayer meeting.

The second year passed quickly. Again she signed up for Daily Vacation Bible Schools and camp for the summer. This time she went to Wisconsin. After the summer ministry she again went home to help her dad with field work.

The Lord found a better maid job for her during her senior year. She worked for Mr. and Mrs. Richard Relf. Mrs. Relf was a nurse and was very kind.

Because of the war Helen Jean decided to go on to seminary. That meant she must take first year Greek. In the first six weeks she received an A in Greek and an F in English 7 and 8. Before the semester was over she would have to raise that to a D. How could she get a C to bring it up?

Again the Lord gave wisdom and help to learn what was needed to finish the course. Years later she compared the two teachers. How different they were! The Greek teacher was a great encourager. She loved her students and took time to explain if they were having trouble. Her English teacher had a love for students, but mostly for those who were at the top of the class. She had written the course so thought it needed no explanation. Just get to work and learn it. Helen Jean desired to graduate so really went to work.

The seniors were honored by an elegant banquet. For the banquets her first and second years she had worn a long yellow gown and decided she was not too proud to wear it again. Mrs. Relf thought otherwise. Her daughter had a closet full of gowns. She could wear any one she liked. The daughter was in the east going to college. Helen Jean picked out one but Mrs. Relf said that would not do for a senior. She picked out a lovely blue one for her. Wah! Helen Jean felt like a queen in it. The time came for her to go to the banquet and Mrs. Relf came out with a lovely corsage of rose colored roses and baby's breath. She had asked her son to take her to the place of the banquet. Helen Jean assured her she would get a taxi to take her back and she did.

Working for Mrs. Relf

Graduation took place in the huge Minneapolis Municipal Auditorium. Helen Jean wore a white cap and gown. A wealthy lady had given each girl a dozen red roses to carry. She was never told who the lady was.

Again Helen Jean filled her summer with teaching Daily Vacation Bible School and camps, after which she went home to help her Dad with harvest.

In the fall she was off again, but this time to seminary. She would graduate with a B.R.E. if she could get all her work finished by the end of the year which was a big order.

Helen Jean worked afternoons as a nurses' aide in Eitel Hospital. Sometimes she and the head nurse were the only ones on the second floor. There were two big wards and ten single rooms. She stayed in the nurses' aide building and ate in the nurses' dining room. She noticed two student dietitians. One of them, Louise Margueling, had a smile all the time. The nurses' aides nicknamed her "Smiles."

Helen Jean and Smiles became good friends. There were special meetings in the Swedish Baptist Church. A group of the nurses' aides who were going to Bible School and Helen Jean decided to go. They invited Smiles to go with them. Praise the Lord that night Smiles became a Christian.

Louise "Smiles" Margueling

When Helen Jean had saved money for Bible school, she had planned for three years. So by seminary there wasn't enough for tuition. The nurses' aide job, however, paid better so by saving she was able to leave debt free after graduation.

Graduation took place again in the Minneapolis Municipal Auditorium. Mrs. Riley herself paid for the roses the seminary girls carried. They wore black caps and gowns. She received a Bachelor of Religious Education.

The crowning blessing of Helen Jean's graduation was to meet her dad and grandmother back stage after graduation. She could not go home with them for she had signed up for Daily Vacation Bible School and camps again. She would return later to help her dad.

Chapter 10
Teaching Again

After coming home from camp Helen Jean realized the war was hindering travel in China at this time. She really did not know what the Lord wanted her to do. Her dad knew exactly what she should do. He contacted the County Superintendent to see his daughter.

The lady was desperate for a teacher. A school close to the Canadian border had had only two or three months of school that year because there just were not enough teachers available.

This year there was plenty of rain. Field work was at a standstill. The Moose farm was half mile off a gravel road with a connecting mud road. When the County Superintendent heard of a teacher she drove to the gravel road and walked the half-mile in the mud.

When she arrived she met Helen Jean and was certain this was a good place for her. This school was made up of mainly Russian people. There was an empty church up there where she could minister to the people on the weekends.

Helen Jean could not help with the field work due to the hindrance of the rain. She decided to take the school.

Dad drove her up there with all her baggage. She would have to board a couple of miles away from the school but as soon as the McCabin home was finished she could board there. This may seem hard to walk two miles each way, but the Lord planned this so that Helen Jean would meet the Hanson family. Mrs. Hanson was an officer of the Farmers Union and had the names and addresses of most of the people of the area. She gave this gold mine of information to Helen Jean and she invited them to church and the school activities.

The church sorely needed a paint job inside, so on Saturdays Helen Jean painted Sunday school rooms.

She had six grades in school. Many of her students were behind in their grades but she filled the black boards with questions and helps each day of school.

She loved her students and had a happy time with them. If they failed to do as they should she would have them bring armfuls of wood to the entryway of school. A couple of older fellows decided to end this detail and piled the entry on both sides with wood so there was only a narrow space to walk into the school.

When Christmas came they had a big Christmas program at church presented by the school. One of the boys cut a tree too tall for the church but they cut it off so it just fit the ceiling. There were no decorations so they whipped up a box of Lux soap. They covered the tree with it so it looked like snow. It was a beauty.

After the program was over Helen Jean expected her dad to come after her but he did not. She had to spend Christmas alone. Because of this she realized that the Lord was more important than her family.

After Christmas she received a letter from her mother to come home. She needed to help Grandma Butler in Iowa. Dad needed a cook for it was an open winter and they could reap many of the fields, which were not combined. Helen Jean had no car but friends took her to the bus station in Lancaster and she was able to get home.

Helen Jean cooked for the hired hands. After vacation she went back to teaching.

One of the local people had a friend who died. Helen Jean sang for the funeral, which was held in the Swedish Baptist Church in Lancaster, Minnesota. This was the first introduction of this church to her. After school was out she was invited to teach DVBS with a friend, Joyce Sjodin. They stayed with the pastor and his wife. After the closing program they stayed over to hear the special speaker. He told them of Paul Hartford's flying school.

There were two things yet Helen Jean wanted to learn before she went to China. She desired to learn to fly for there were not means of communication in China where she wanted to go. The other ambition was to learn to translate the Bible. She knew that in that area they did not have the written Word in their language.

She immediately applied to the flying school and was accepted for the fall enrollment at Victory Sky Pilots.

Chapter 11
Flying School

Most people who had heard about Helen Jean going to flying school thought that she had gone crazy. However, the Lord dealt with Helen Jean so she knew this is what the Lord wanted her to do.

In August of 1945 she took a bus to Winona Lake, Indiana. Victory Sky Pilots had its headquarters in the Garfield Hotel in Winona Lake. There she met the president of the school, Rev. Paul Hartford.

At school she found several people who were planning to go to the mission field. Only one had been on the mission field for a term.

Rev. Demy and his wife were home from Liberia. They were missionaries under the mission, which was then called Mid-Missions. Years later, in 1952, he mission adopted the nickname as Baptist Mid-Missions.

Rev. Daniel Feryance was working on his birth certificate so he could take his solo test. He had worked all summer to get proof that he was born here in the United States. He was born at home rather than in a hospital so there was no hospital record. His mother had a lady help as midwife so there was no doctor's report. He used Sunday school records as well as school records. In the end, with a testimony of a friend who knew his mother, he received his birth certificate.

Helen Jean's mother had recorded her birth. However, before they settled on a name for Helen Jean the record had to be sent into the courthouse, so she was known as Baby Moose until the time she was in flying school. In a very short while that seemed too long to Helen Jean, she had her correct birth certificate.

Shortly after Helen Jean arrived on August 8, 1945, the president of the school took her flying. He did many things to show off his flying ability. He took her through double eights. Poor Helen Jean's head was about to burst. When she got down on the ground she wondered whether the Lord really wanted her to fly.

A fellow-student, Mr. Melvin Wymuth, noticed Helen Jean and encouraged her. He let her know flying yourself would not cause her head to ache. If she were flying herself she could land before she felt bad.

Helen Jean as the human starter motor

Every day the weather permitted, the students went to the airport early in the morning. The wind built up by noon so they were back to the dorm for the noon meal. If the weather was good they again went to the airport around 4 o'clock. There were not enough airplanes to go around so Helen Jean waited for her turn. She had an army instructor who was loved by all his students. Joe encouraged and helped the students to learn the right way to fly and the safe way. He could be calm in the toughest of situations. He had Helen Jean solo on October 24, 1945. This was a great day for now she could go to the airport and log in and out to practice without an instructor.

At night they had ground school. They studied weather patterns, rules for flying in the United States, and instructions for good flying. Often the night ended by what they called "hanger flying". This meant telling of some experience that they recently had which might help the rest of the students. After this, good advice was handed out to the students.

The students each had a big book of rules with questions and answers in it. This was put out by the government. Every student had to take a test over the whole book before they could be graduated.

Helen Jean soon became the teacher for each who had to take their test. While she was waiting at the airport she would help those who were not flying. She saw her students pass but most of all she was also learning the rules for the time when she would have to take the test.

Helen Jean felt God had called her to China. She, however, had not found a mission board. She had talked to Mrs. Charles Cowman, who then had a number of missionaries in China. Mrs. Cowman was very kind. She told her that her thinking was not like her mission. She was Methodist. She sensed immediately that Helen Jean was Baptist. At first Helen Jean was disappointed, but she applied for a passport. When she received it immediately she was encouraged to go to China.

Rev. and Mrs. Demy suggested she go under Mid-Missions. As a result, while in flying school, she wrote the mission and received some papers to fill out concerning what she believed. She filled these out and sent them to Cleveland, Ohio. She was soon invited to appear before its council at Mishawaka, Indiana. She could fly up there but the day came with a strong wind. She decided to take the bus.

When she arrived at the church, the church was filled with missionaries from Africa. She was about ready to leave and go back to flying school when the council called her to meet them in a room in the basement of the church.

When she arrived in the room, it was filled with men who looked like big business men. They asked her many questions. The last question they asked her was "Would you be willing to go to Africa?" She said, "No, if you can not send me to China I must find another mission board." With that she walked out.

As she walked upstairs she had no hope they would accept her. However, word quickly came. She was accepted in February of 1946, but she would have to wait for someone to go with her. In the meantime they invited her, after graduation from flying school, to come and work in the home office of the mission.

God had answered prayer. Now she had a mission. Now she must graduate from flying school. She could not possibly know of the testings which were yet before her.

Chapter 12
God's Protection

Flying takes a lot of money. Shortly after soloing Helen Jean realized she did not have enough money to finish the training to graduate from flying school.

Mrs. Hartford was the cook for the flying school. She needed to be away for a while and the school needed a cook. Helen Jean immediately applied and became the cook during Mrs. Hartford's absence. After Mrs. Hartford came back Helen Jean applied to be a nurses' aide at the nearby McDonald hospital. The doctor's wife was the head nurse. She encouraged Helen Jean's going to the mission field and taught her much about practical medical work.

When the weather was good she would fly in the morning and work as a nurses' aide in the afternoons.

Every flyer must take a cross-country trip. One must land in three places and get the logbook signed.

The day came when Helen Jean was to take her cross-country. Joe helped her map out her flight plan. Her first stop would be in Fort Wayne, Indiana. She would then hop to Marion, Indiana, and her last stop would be home base at Warsaw, Indiana.

Helen Jean, prayed, checked her plane and then told Joe that the wind seemed to be too strong. He thought it would be okay. He told her to be sure and gas up in Marion after she had her logbook signed.

Off she went. She stopped at Fort Wayne and got her logbook signed and took off for Marion. Wah! She had to go straight into the wind. Little did she know how quickly the wind was using up her gas. About three miles out from Marion the engine stopped. Helen Jean looked around for a place to land. There were three choices. She missed the first one, but set down nicely in the second one which was a pasture. The engine seemed to be okay, but the gas tank was empty! Her tank of praise to God was overflowing!

She walked to a nearby farmhouse and asked if they had any high-octane gas. They assured her the gas they had would work, for recently another plane had come down there and they had helped them.

The man helped Helen Jean gas up. She checked the plane over to be sure that everything was in order and to her knowledge it was. She was only a little ways from the next airport where she would stop.

"Gas it up and go!"

She took off leaving all the good landing places behind her when the engine stopped again. This time there was a wooded area on the side and a cornfield below. This time she would have to come down in a stall. If the plane veered off course it would become a pile of junk and perhaps a coffin. As she came down ears of corn hit the nose of the ship and made two small dents. There was not a scratch that could be found any place else on the ship. Helen Jean was very much alive, and the plane was in one piece. Only God could do this!

She phoned Joe, so he and Rev. Hartford came in another plane. They also brought gas for the plane.

Helen Jean didn't want to fly anymore, but Joe encouraged her. He did not realize the Lord had enabled her to set down safely in that cornfield without a scratch.

However, the bad news was that she would have to take another cross-country flight. Joe insisted she come to the airport the next day and fly. At first she was fearful but Philippians 4:13 is still in the Bible as a needed reminder that she could do all things through Christ.

The day came when Joe encouraged her to take her test from the government. He first took her up and checked all the patterns she would have in the test. When she did the spin her head felt funny, but she came out of it quite well.

The runway was crossed by two mud puddles. Joe said she should set the wheels of the plane on the dry ground between the puddles and take off before the second puddle. He would check the plane to see if there was mud or water on the plane when she got down. Again Joe was in for a shock. There was no mud or water on the plane. Again only the Lord could have helped her accomplish that!

After they came down and checked the plane Joe started to chew out Helen Jean, up one side and down the other. He had never done this before. He had always encouraged her. He did not want his students to go before the government inspector with a proud look.

Helen Jean went back to the place where she stayed feeling beat. Joe said she was a poor flyer. How could she ever pass the test?

She went to her room and fell on her knees. She poured out her heart to the Lord when her little New Testament which she carried fell out of her pocket of her shirt. It opened to the front page:

Helen Jean Moose
"I can do all things through Christ, which strengtheneth me."
Phil. 4:13

Wah! After tomorrow she would have to put "except fly a plane" after the verse. But the verse didn't say that. Christ would strengthen her. He surely would help her as He had done before. The verse gave her peace and assurance that she would pass with His strength. She went to bed and slept like a log through the night. The next day she passed her test, praise the Lord!

Helen Jean was the first girl to get her wings from Victory Sky Pilots. How she praised the Lord, for the next stop would be in Cleveland, Ohio, to work in the home office of Mid-Missions on her way to China.

Chapter 13
The Home Office

After graduating from Victory Sky Pilots Helen Jean went to the home office of Baptist Mid-Missions which was located in Cleveland, Ohio.

Her job description was simple: help anywhere she was needed. She found Mrs. Barrett a vital role model for her. Mrs. Barrett was the wife of Mr. Charles Barrett, a former soap manufacturer. He was a godly man who never wasted time and expected that of his workers also. The Lord used him mightily, not only in the home office, but also in his church, which was Hough Avenue Baptist Church. He wrote music for his choir.

After Daniel Feryance was graduated from Victory Sky Pilots he and Arthur Summerville came to Cleveland. They had their passports and were on their way to Europe for an evangelistic trip. They came to see Helen Jean at the home office. She again suggested that they go under a mission board. As a result they went to see Mr. George Milner, the president of the mission at that time. Shortly after that there was a mission conference and the two of them were accepted as the first missionaries to Europe under Baptist Mid-Missions.

One day Papa Barrett called Helen Jean into his office. He told her there was a church in Winterset, Iowa, that wanted a missionary speaker. Would she go? She would receive no money for it was a very small church. She should have a round trip ticket if she went by bus. This she could do so off she went.

When she got off the bus Rev. Shute met her and said we can't give you any money. She surprised him by saying, "That doesn't matter, I have a round trip ticket." He was relieved.

That night she spoke, and the Lord blessed in a real way. Two young people gave their lives for full time service. Later she heard they went to the mission field. Later this little church took Helen Jean on as a missionary and has been a faithful church through the years.

After the service was over she stayed overnight with Mr. and Mrs. Hircocks. The next day she was on her way back to the home office.

Faithfully she did whatever she could in the mission office. Sometimes she helped with the mailing, which at that time was not more than 400 letters to churches. She also learned how to wrap books for overseas missionaries.

One day she was asked to file. There was a huge pile of paperwork to be filed for it had not been done for some time. After the pile was down part way she came on to a letter telling about a summer session offering lessons on translation of the Bible sponsored by Wycliffe. Wah! There was still time to go if she could be released from the home office. She went to Papa Barrett and asked his advice. He thought it was a good idea to take the training. So she applied, and soon received a letter stating she was approved as a student for their summer Linguistics course.

Helen Jean had just enough money for the bus ticket and part of her school fees. She would depend on the Lord to help her raise enough money for the rest.

When she arrived at Norman, Oklahoma, she had only her carry-on luggage. All the rest was lost. For one month she had to sleep in part of her clothes and wash the rest by hand to keep up with the hot weather.

Every day she looked for her luggage to arrive. Daily she seemed less hopeful of ever receiving it. What a situation it was, going to school in the same clothes day after day. However, she praised the Lord they stood the wear.

After about a month word came from the bus depot to come get her luggage. God had answered prayer. What a praise party took place!

If God could do the impossible in getting her luggage back surely He could pay her school fees somehow.

"On the road again..."

A few days before the summer session ended one of the work leaders asked for help to clean rooms. You would be paid. This was good news to Helen Jean. Immediately she set to work cleaning a big room in her spare time.

The work was not easy in the warm room, but she kept going. She was nearly done with one room when she heard footsteps. In came Leola Barum, a missionary under her mission. She had been stationed in India. She asked Helen Jean what she was doing so she explained how she was paying her school bill. Leola asked her how much she owed. Helen Jean confessed she absolutely had no money. She would have to work for her school bill and a bus ticket home. Leola left Helen Jean to her misery and came back with a handful of bills saying, "This is my tithe, which has been piling up for some needy missionary and it has your name on it."

Again the Lord had answered prayer. Again she could only praise Him. Philippians 4:13 was proven true one more time.

Chapter 14
Deputation

When Helen Jean was studying in Norman, Oklahoma, Baptist Mid-Missions accepted another person for the China field. This was good news and bad news for Helen Jean. Miss Violet LaFever felt led to work in Shanghai on the coast of China. She had a desire to start an orphanage. But Helen Jean felt God had called her to go interior where city after city had no church, and where they did not have a Bible in their tongue.

But was God's will for Helen Jean to work on the coast? She started on deputation planning to leave as soon as possible. Helen Jean had gone home to see her parents and pack when a phone call came from Violet. She was leaving right away and wanted Helen Jean to go immediately. Helen Jean told her she did not have all her support and that she could not leave now. Violet let her know she should trust the Lord and go <u>now!</u> Violet left for China without Helen Jean.

Later Helen Jean learned Violet left Baptist Mid-Missions after she had been in China only a short time. Helen Jean could only praise the Lord that the lack of support saved her from a bad situation.

Helen Jean continued her deputation and was told she needed to be a member of a G.A.R.B. Church. Calvary Baptist Church in Forest City, Iowa was the nearest to her home. They had taken on some of her support so she applied and became a member there. This church has been a faithful church to her throughout her missionary life.

Shortly after this Helen Jean heard of her classmate from Northwestern Bible School who, when they were seated alphabetically, would sit side-by-side in most classes. Her name was Helen Miles.

At the time she was a home missionary working in Fargo, North Dakota. She invited Helen Jean to speak to her work. When the invitation was given Helen Miles herself felt led to give her life for China. She applied to Baptist Mid-Missions and was accepted.

The two of them went to the West Coast with Rev. Paul Metzler. While out there they decided to apply for their visas. In order to do this they had to have a medical examination. Helen Miles did not want to do this. She would apply later. After some meetings they went back to the midwest, Helen Miles to Colorado and Helen Jean to Minnesota.

When Helen Miles was in Colorado she met an old boy friend who told her she did not believe the doctrine of Baptist Mid-Missions. Jesus was not coming back anytime but that was far in the future. As a result she resigned from the mission and married the fellow.

Again Helen Jean was without someone to go to China with her. What was the Lord trying to tell her? She kept on having meetings and passed through Minneapolis, Minnesota, where Louise Marqueling was a dietitian at St. Barnabas Hospital and found she had gone to Bible school. She was planning to be a missionary. She had come to know the Lord when the girls from Eitel Hospital and Helen Jean had taken her to some special meetings at the First Swedish Baptist Church.

Louise applied to Baptist Mid-Missions and was accepted for China. She resigned her position from St. Barnabas and they rented a third floor flat for the summer. They called it the dusty pink apartment. Louise and Helen Jean could share the apartment and go to meetings from there. They decided to wallpaper the apartment since it was much in need of a fresh new look. They immediately did the job and it felt clean again. They piled their footlockers up to divide the huge room into four rooms. The bathroom was down the hall. They rented this for the summer, sub-leasing it from students who went to Bible school in the winter.

Dr. Joseph Stowell had a friend at Yale University who was the head of one of the divisions of the Far Eastern language department at Yale. They taught Korean, Japanese and Chinese. Mr. Cox was head of the Chinese department.

The girls applied and were accepted for language school. When they arrived in New Haven, Connecticut, they looked for an apartment but found that all the Yale students had taken them. They found only a room and they had to eat their meals downtown at the "Y" and this was very costly. They could not continue doing this, but what should they do? They heard about the Alliance Church (the only fundamental church in New Haven at that time) having a prayer meeting. Helen Jean suggested that they go, but Louise was tired from house hunting so Helen Jean went by herself. They asked for testimonies at the meeting and Helen Jean gave a testimony. After the service was over Mrs. Sarjen, a Ukranian lady, invited her to look at a third floor apartment. She was a Christian and gave it to them at an affordable rent. They lived there for the rest of the time they were at Yale.

Louise and Helen Jean at the
sound scriber at Yale

Both were put in the top class of the Chinese classes. One night Helen Jean dreamed she was put in the lowest class of the Chinese classes. She awoke and felt so badly. She did not know God was preparing her for a blow very soon. It was not long in coming. She was challenged to really work. This challenged the others to do likewise. A warm winter coat was a welcome gift from her father.

Learning to write characters was not too hard for her but to remember which stroke came first proved to be a problem. Both of the girls had to work like beavers for many of the students were bright government students with high motivation.

During her vacations while studying at Yale, Louise was able to raise all her support. They planned to go to China after graduation but the longshoremen's strike prevented any ships from leaving from the West Coast. It was too costly to sail to China from the East Coast.

Winter coats keep Helen Jean and Louise warm at Yale.

Chapter 15
Waiting

After graduating from the Far Eastern Language School at Yale University on June 4, 1948, Louise Marqueling and Helen Jean Moose expected to leave soon for China. Their dreams were shattered by the Longshoremen's strike on the West Coast.

In those days strikes were settled in a couple of weeks or so. However, the girls were in for a long wait. They decided to stay in New Haven for a few weeks. They helped with the DVBS. When it was over the strike still had shipping at a standstill.

Near to the apartment was a black family with their many friends. They were not welcome in those days at the white churches in New Haven. Louise and Helen Jean decided to have a DVBS just for them.

Mrs. Sarajian told them they could use the barn in back since it was not being used at the time. They swept it and dressed it up, making it look like a very inviting room. Big and little black children came. For one week the old barn was a happy place for all who came.

Louise and Helen Jean realized they must leave New Haven to get to the West Coast before there was no more space on the ship for them to go to China.

After leaving New Haven they visited their supporting churches along the way. Being alert, however, to the progress of the strike, they went from church to church.

Finally, on August 24, 1948 they arrived in Salina, Kansas, where Louise's folks lived. While there, they prepared Story-o-Graph figures to be used with children's work. They made all that was produced by that company. They colored, cut out, and pasted flannel on the back. They bagged them, putting a small picture of what the story contained. This took all the time they had between meetings and going to the dentist.

On September 13 Louise made her grandma happy by baking a birthday cake with 86 candles. "My! She was old!" the girls thought. Her birthday was not until October 6, but the girls were fearful they would be gone by that time.

After the Mission Council had met they decided to suggest that the girls consider another field. The letter arrived after they had been invited to go to the West Coast to stay with Rev. and Mrs. Larson.

What should they do? They both agreed to send a telegram and leave for the West Coast. But, What should they say? They had to say what they wanted to say in ten words or less.

After some time Louise came up with, "Devil always hindering". That was not long enough so Helen Jean added, "Please, don't help him". Imagine two dumb girls sending such a telegram! Nevertheless, they thought, come what may, they had been hindered long enough.

On November 29 the girls received a letter from the mission with permission to proceed.

They had moved to the Home of Peace which helped them buy tickets, food, and things for the trip. Soon the strike was over.

On December 15th the girls were helped aboard the "General Meigs", a converted troop ship. They were given bunks in the officers' quarters.

Rev. Larson's church and young people came to see them off. They tossed things up to them on the ship. Both of the girls had their hands full of paper streamers, which broke when the ship moved out to sea. They had broken ties with their homeland to venture into the sunset.

Leaving America was a happy time but a sad time. Would they ever be able to return and see their loved ones again? God had called them. He would comfort them. He surely did!

Chapter 16
On Board Ship

In the officers' quarters of the "USS General Meigs" there were bunks four in a stack. Louise found her bunk on the floor level, but Helen Jean's was four bunks up. They put their things on the bed and went for dinner in the dining room.

When they returned after the dinner they found a Chinese lady sitting on Louise's bed. Louise asked her if that was her bunk. She said it was not. Her bunk was four bunks up and she could not climb. Immediately Louise struck up a bargain with her. She would trade bunks with her if she was willing. The Chinese lady was so grateful. Louise climbed up four bunks just opposite Helen Jean. Praise the Lord! They were much safer up there than on ground level.

This was December 14, 1948, but they would not arrive in Shanghai, China, before December 31 if all went well.

The ship was loaded with Oriental people and missionaries. After the evening meal many of the Orientals would play in the lobby a game that resembled dominos and was called mahjong. They used this game to gamble.

Many of the Overseas Fellowship missionaries had children. To be cooped up in the ship was really boring to them. Louise and Helen Jean went to the ship officers and asked if they could have a Bible Club for them. They were glad for any help in making the children happy. As a result they had a Bible Club for the children when there were no sights to see and the girls felt good.

December 18 the ship had an aloha supper for many who would disembark in Hawaii the next day. A travel agent came aboard and made an announcement. She would help anyone interested to see the sights in Hawaii for only $20.00. She did not say anything about going to church and it was Sunday.

Louise and Helen Jean decided to get off and find a church. They were walking wobbly from being on the ship for five days but decided do or die they were going to church.

They were taken to a phone booth by a big lorry truck. They looked in the phone book for a church nearby. They found the Salvation Army was just a little ways off so they went there. There were all of eight people present. Poinsettias were as tall as the first story of the building in the driveway. They were lovely red ones. What a sight! After the service they decided to take a streetcar and go as far as they could, then go the other way as far as they could. They spent two dimes altogether apiece, much better than any $20 tour.

On the way back they passed a park where they heard the song "No, Never Alone". Helen Jean suggested they get off and see who was making the music. Louise did not seem to think it wise but after a bit they got off and walked back to the park.

The Southern Baptists were having an outdoor service. There they met Cora Pardon, a single missionary who invited them to her home.

She introduced them to the fruit of papaya and guava. She asked the girls what they had seen but decided she could show them many more interesting sights and did.

She took them to early church where they were having a Christmas program with a Chinese girl as Mary the mother of Jesus. What a blessed service it was! It was early enough so the girls could get back on the ship on time.

After the service was over Cora drove them to see a few more sights on the way to the ship. What a wonderful day thanks to Cora and her friendship.

When they arrived on board ship, the girls found a wealthy Christian Indian lady who had taken the expensive tour. She suffered from a sore back and her feet developed uncomfortable spots from walking. She was disappointed at spending so much money and receiving so little.

The girls however were testifying what a wonderful time they had had in the Lord's house twice, seeing a Christmas program and spending all of two dimes each! They had experienced so much of the real life of the people. The blessings were added to them because they sought the Lord first.

Chapter 17
Landing

On December 21, 1948, Louise Marqueling and Helen Jean received permission to hold a Bible club class once a day while sailing. That first afternoon fifteen children came. Three children expressed a desire to become Christians after Louise told the story of the rich man and Lazarus.

On the very next day they met Sgt. Jacob DeShazer who was returning to Japan as a missionary. He had been shot down during the war and taken as a prisoner for 40 months. Of those months 34 of them had been spent in solitary confinement in Japan.

His general was General Jimmy Dolittle over a squadron of sixteen B–25 bombers. All sixteen aircraft crashed and were lost. The crew of Sgt. DeShazer's plane was forced to parachute into Japanese-held territory. He was taken prisoner right away. Three of his crew members were killed, while another crew member died of starvation before their eyes.

While he was in prison he was given books and even a Bible. After reading the Bible and realizing the value of it on June 8, 1944, he became a Christian. His whole life changed. The people he had hated he now loved. Those over him saw a great change in his life.

When the war finally ended in August of 1945 he was returned to the U. S. where he immediately studied to be a missionary to Japan. In Bible school he met and married Florence.

According to Southern California Christian Times, "He spent 30 years in Japan as a missionary and saw 23 churches started. Sometimes he spoke five times in one day."

Christmas Eve on the top bunk of the officers' quarters of the "USS General Meigs" was a lonely spot for Helen Jean, so far from home and family. There were no Christmas trimmings and she had just one package she had brought from Mother to be opened on Christmas Eve. She shed a few tears and went to sleep.

December 28, 1948 Sgt. Jacob DeShazer, Florence and little Paul left the ship in Japan to start their great lifework. Louise and Helen Jean continued their journey. Their first sight of China was on the final day of 1948, at the coastal city of Shanghai. However, they were going to Hong Kong so still had a few more days left before they would walk like wobbly sailors on dry land.

The dazzled young ladies were welcomed in Hong Kong on January 3, 1949, by Rev. and Mrs. Krug and three children, two of whom were sick. Taking thirty three pieces of luggage through customs and getting off to Kweilin was no small job for two girls who had never had such an experience. But the Lord directed, and the Krugs took them to New Asia Hotel for the night.

Rev. Krug and family
in Hong Kong

About midnight they awoke to gunfire. Both girls got up and stood near the window and peeked out. Wah! It was just a long strip of firecrackers burning and popping!

The Lord had said, "Fear not".

Chapter 18
China at Last!

One of the first things Helen Jean had to do when she arrived in Hong Kong was to renew her passport. She had felt it unwise to get it renewed before she left America in case paperwork held it up so she could not sail when the ship was ready.

Bookings were difficult to obtain since so many people had long been waiting for a ticket. Helen Jean had decided to trust the Lord to let her ship arrive in time to renew her passport in Hong Kong. She praised the Lord when her passport was renewed by just paying the usual fee. The next item of business was to cable a message to the Home Office that they had arrived safely.

Rev. Krug suggested the thirty-three pieces of luggage be forwarded to Canton at Dr. Chyang's hospital where they would stay before boarding the train to go north.

Both Louise and Helen Jean had made lists of what each footlocker or box contained. One footlocker was filled with medicine. Each time they were inspected they would show them the lists of each piece. They then would pray that if the inspectors opened any footlocker or box it would not be the medicine. Praise the Lord. He answers prayer.

One suitcase of Helen Jean's had a vitamin bottle with three or four pills in it. They opened the bottle in such a manner that they fell on the floor. One of the inspectors asked if she wanted the vitamins. She said, "No". When others were not looking he quickly ate them.

While waiting for the train in Canton, China to go up country with the Krugs, Louise decided to leave her set of dishes there at the hospital. It was in a box by itself. They also left tools that would not be needed for the present.

They arrived in Kweilin on January 13. It was cold. Most houses had no heat unless you had a stove for cooking. Many homes did not have a stove but a pot of burning charcoal, and both Louise and Helen Jean came down with bad colds. Later in the month on they heard that Nanking fell to the Red army and that it was advancing even closer to Kweilin.

The Krugs had lived in a store building. They hoped to rent a home when the girls came and rent them a room. After the girls came they went looking at the rented places but found none. As a result the girls were put up in the storeroom where the trunks were stored.

The girls found a clearing in this large room near the windows. They put their footlockers in a pile forming a wall for their bedroom. There was no ceiling so you could look up and see tile roof and beams to tie the walls together.

On one side the wall was boarded. On the other side was another store where men gambled at night. You could hear them moving their mahjong dominoes and occasionally shouting something they could not understand. Maybe that was just as well.

The girls had brought army cots and air mattresses with a pump. The pump blew up the mattress quickly. They had plenty of bedding in their luggage. As a result they were nice and warm in bed. Each of them had a flashlight, which she kept handy beside her bed.

Deep in the first night there was strange noise. When they heard a noise they would flash their lights in that direction. Often the noise was from a rat on the roof trying to find a loose tile that would let them in. Often the rat would leave if caught in the light. Sometimes they would run on the beam across the room. The girls soon found that sleeping under a mosquito net was far more comforting than sleeping exposed to the local wildlife.

By the end of March the girls discovered the source of unwanted aromas: a dead rat in the corner of their room. It soon had a funeral but the procession bypassed the kitchen. They could do without rat soup.

The girls had already started language school in late January of 1949. They needed to know Bible words and other vocabulary for their gospel lessons. Often they would take their visual aids of a story to class and learn the words for it.

The Southern Baptists had a good language school in Kweilin so they applied to study there. Dr. Chyang was a good teacher and really loved the Lord. He helped the girls a lot.

Dr. Chyang, a fine teacher of Mandarin

Miss Lyou also taught there. She was not a Christian. One day Helen Jean showed her the English Bible which she brought from America. Helen Jean explained that if you believed the Bible it was a powerful book. When Helen Jean was not looking the teacher slipped it into her bag. That night Helen Jean could not find her Bible. What a loss! After several days the Bible mysteriously reappeared. Miss Lyou had not found the kind of power in it she was seeking!

Every day the girls studied but they needed a warmer place and a place of quietness. They hired a man to make a bamboo structure inside the warehouse near their beds. They papered it with grass paper. They papered the top so there was a roof. The electric light came down in about the middle of the room. One side had a window with a nice curtain.

They each bought a desk and chair. One chair and desk cost about $1.25 in U. S. dollars. They could afford that. They also bought a small stove. At last they were comfortable! The Lord was good. They finished their lovely study on February 13 as a wonderful valentine from the Lord.

The study was just above the room that served as a store. This was the area without chairs where Rev. Krug showed slides every night to the people who were interested in the Bible. Often the room was full of people. He spoke Cantonese and a teenage girl named Aloha interpreted it into Kweilin Chinese, a dialect of Mandarin.

On February 22nd Louise and Helen Jean started a Sunday school for the children on the wall of the city. This helped them to learn the language by using it in real life situations. Louise was good at this. Their language school teachers helped them speak so the children could understand them. What a joy to finally be doing the Lord's work in China.

Sunday School children in Kweilin

Chapter 19
On The Move For The Lord

The Communists were coming down from North China into Kweilin. Rev. Krug was not well. Mrs. Krug would soon have a baby, and Philip, the oldest of their children, was sickly. In Kweilin there were not many people who spoke Cantonese, the only Chinese language that the Krugs spoke. As a family they decided to go to Canton where they had a Chinese doctor friend. Dr. Chyang had a large hospital in Canton and welcomed any Chinese Christian workers while they were in Canton.

Dr. Chyang's hospital in Canton

Mrs. Chyang with Louise Margueling

May 6, 1949, Louise Marqueling and Helen Jean Moose found themselves selling things to reduce their luggage, as well as other articles the Krugs wanted to sell. With much sorrow Louise and Helen had to leave Kweilin with the Krugs.

After they all arrived in Canton, Rev. and Mrs. Krug told the girls they were going back to America. This decision came as quite a shock to the girls. They immediately cabled the mission to see if they could stay in China. The return cable affirmed their clearance to remain in China..

The girls knew that very few people in Canton could understand their Chinese for they spoke Mandarin not Cantonese. Both girls prayed about their next steps. Helen Jean felt led to go interior as close to Tibet as possible. To go interior might mean never to come out alive again; but God had called her and she knew she must follow. After praying and knowing God's will Louise also felt the Lord's leading to the interior of China.

The next step was to find a plane that would fly interior. Because of the danger of a plane being shot down over the area, which was now governed by the Red Army, there were many airline ticket offices that were not selling tickets. However, one agent suggested trying the Lutheran plane office, which flew the St. Paul. The girls immediately went and found that the St. Paul was loaded with half a load of bicycles but they needed a half load more. That was not a problem for the girls. They had half a plane load of footlockers. The plane was bound for Chengdu where the girls wanted to go.

In the dark of night on July 21st the St. Paul safely arrived in Chengdu with a half load of bikes, a half load of footlockers, Captain, co-pilot and two missionary ladies who were laden with uncertainty about everything except that God had directed them there. The captain of the St. Paul was a kind man. After seeing that no one met the girls at the airport he informed them that he always stayed at the Canadian Mission and suggested they go with him and his co-pilot. In the morning they could find their own place to live.

Helen Jean and Louise fly to Chengdu
on the "Saint Paul."

They found a train of rickshaws to take their luggage through the heavy rain with water up on the wheels of the rickshahs, and arrived at the Canadian Mission wet and with plenty of luggage. The mission was willing to give them a place to sleep and a place for their luggage but they were expected to move in the morning.

The girls went to bed rejoicing and expected the Lord to do great things in the morning.

Chapter 20
War on the Way

Louise and Helen Jean, after a good night of sleep, went seeking for a place to live. They found that the Conservative Baptist missionaries had a large room they would rent. However, soon they were leaving for western China and had to give up the place at that time. The girls hoped to find a place of their own in a few days so that was not a problem.

In the mean time they must go to language school to change their dialect to Szechwan Chinese of five tones from four tones which they had learned.

June 26, 1949 the girls started language school. Dr. Moncrof had them review the Bryant book, which was simple, compared to the work at Yale. He also decided that girls should learn little sound marks beside the characters to tell how they sounded and what tone the character had.

They were able to buy Chinese Bibles with these sound marks beside each character. The Bible was three inches thick on thin paper with good-sized characters. Helen Jean bought one and put all the sound marks on the flyleaves of the Bible, with the English sound. When she was in doubt about the sound she could quickly look it up in her Bible.

A dear old Chinese Methodist pastor named Pastor Pan taught the girls the words in the Chinese Bible. His Chinese was outstanding.

They worked first on the events of the life of Christ. Later they worked on book after book of the Bible.

Shortly after they were settled in language school they heard that Mrs. Edwards, a Chinese teacher they had at Yale, was right there in Chengdu.

After a search they found she was in the hospital. The food was terrible and since the baby girl had come she had not had a bath. Helen Jean put to use her skill as a nurse's aide to help her feel much better with a bath and a better bed.

By August 12 Helen Jean passed thirteen chapters of Bryant's textbook for Dr. Moncrof. Ever so slowly were the five tones becoming a part of the girls' speech.

Then on August 13 Manham fell to the Reds. This place was not too far away. Only five days later the American Consulate announced they were packing and going home. They suggested that all Americans do likewise. However, if any chose not to leave, the British Consul would help them with legal papers.

Almost every morning a bell would ring outside, and the girls could look out and see cloths spread on the porch or lawn filled with things to sell. The Chinese loved to bargain with you if they thought you were interested in an article.

August 17, 1949 Helen Jean bought four lovely pieces of silk work called "Four Seasons" and sent them home to her mother. Her mother had them framed as art works and hung them in her living room. After her death they were returned to Helen Jean. They are still hanging in her dining room at Missionary Acres as reminders of those blessed days.

Many of the missionaries that they knew now left for America as soon as they could obtain their legal papers. All but one family of the TEAM Mission who were in Chengdu departed. The Canadian missionaries left as soon as possible.

The China Inland Mission, most of whom were Baptists in this area, decided to stay.

A Swedish lady also decided to stay. Louise and Helen Jean had a work they could not leave at that time. This bold Swedish lady, Honey, really loved the Lord and was working up country from Chengdu.

Daily Choices for Christ

One day a soldier came into her humble home and demanded that she give him her table. She looked him straight in the eye and said, "You can't have that table. It belongs to the Lord!" He walked out without the table. After this event Honey realized she must not stay alone so she moved to Chengdu.

August 20 a Noso chieftain came to Chengdu. His name was Lyang Gwan Iyan and he was looking for someone to help his people. Louise and Helen Jean needed more Bible study in Chinese before they could leave.

By this time Louise and Helen Jean had found an empty apartment for rent at $20 a month. It was located on Hwa Si Ba Campus at number 51. It had a huge living room just right for campus outreach ministry.

They bought sawhorse-type benches for $1 each from the TEAM missionaries who were leaving for America. Each bench could hold four children in Bible Club or two young people who were students. They bought 30 benches.

The living room soon became alive with Hwa Si Ba students. One area of the living room was curtained off as a prayer room.

The girls were still working on the language with Pastor Pam but the language school was closed since the people in charge had gone home.

High schools and middle schools wanted the girls to come and help their school learn English. They could have had a ministry of teaching English if they would just leave out the Bible. They felt their work was not English but God's work in the Chinese Bible, and declined the offer.

On Saturday nights the university students came for a service. Many of the songs they sang were Scripture passages set to music. Emily, a Chinese girl who seemed to know many songs, helped Helen Jean greatly. Another girl played Helen Jean's pump organ to liven the singing.

Emily, a big help

One of the students became a Christian and was invited to come to the Saturday meeting. When testimony time came he got up very bashfully and said, "I have been reading my Bible. I have found a most wonderful, wonderful verse but I seem to have a hard time to find it." After some searching he let out a big sound. "Oh! I found it. Let me read it to you!" He read John 3:16. The whole group cheered.

Some of the faithful students

Chapter 21
Noso Chief

Shortly after Louise and Helen Jean had arrived with their luggage in the big room Rev. and Mrs. Bill Simmons had rented them the Simmons had visitors. The visitors proved to be very interesting. A Noso chief and his men wanted to invite missionaries to come to his area. His area was close to Tibet where the girls hoped someday to minister. He seemed to understand the local language, Chengdu Hwa, but did not understand the language the girls spoke which was Peiping Hwa. Rev. and Mrs. Simmons had been studying the local language for some time so could talk to him.

A Noso chief

Within a short time the Simmons left to go near Tibet. The girls found a flat on Hwa Si Ba campus. They determined to study diligently so they could go west as soon as possible.

The girls soon made friends with many young people. Their house became a home for a student center after their language classes were over for the day so they had to study in the morning and early afternoons to accommodate the college students.

Saturday nights they invited all the students to come for a meeting. They were happy to see students from near Tibet come. However, they needed someone to help them understand one another's Chinese. The girls worked diligently on the local Chinese. The westerners worked on English and Gwo Yu the language of the university that the girls spoke. Some of the Christians helped them. The westerners kept coming to the Saturday meetings when they could.

On Sunday the girls liked to attend the China Inland Baptist Church since it was entirely Chinese. Sometimes they did not understand too much but they were learning and progressing.

Well into the fall of the year they noticed some strangers. They looked like westerners. Wah! There was the Noso Chief and a few of his men. He recognized the girls and greeted them, so the girls quickly invited him to have dinner with them. They could not come that day but settled on a day he and his friends could come.

Louise worked with the cook to make a good dinner. They also cooked plenty of rice. The cook did not seem happy to serve such a meal to them. The men arrived and were taken to the dining room, seated about a round table. Thanksgiving was given for the arrival of the men and for the food to the only true God of the world.

The girls rang a bell, the sign for the cook to bring in the feast. He was a little man with a huge tray piled high. The girls will never know what happened next whether the tray was too heavy or the cook stubbed his toe. All they knew was the loaded tray crashed to the floor and the food could not be used! The cook quickly said he was sorry. He would bring in something for them to eat. The mops came out and a pail for the food which littered the floor.

The chief was not bothered too much by the accident for it gave him time to talk to the girls. As they sat around the empty table they found the chief had come for supplies. He was well aware of the war coming closer to Chengdu. If he did come again he and his men would have to become soldiers and he did not want that.

Louise could speak the local Chinese better than Helen Jean so she did most of the talking with the group. Helen Jean enjoyed listening.

After what seemed a long time to the girls, the cook entered with rice, vegetables and tea. The guests politely enjoyed it. The chief then told the girls he would like them to come as soon as possible but they wanted to know the Lord's will on this. They were in need of a good grasp of the local language before they could come. This might well take a year or more.

After the chief left they prayed to the Lord that He would show them what to do. What a difficult problem! Yet the only thing they could do was to struggle on with the language.

When other missionaries were leaving for home for fear of the war the girls could only keep their minds on their studies so they could go west. The war machine came ever closer. They stayed on and still worked on the language.

Word came the Chief was translating the Bible so his people could read it in their language.

After the war came to Chengdu there was no hope of the girls ever going west. They would have to leave as all the rest did. Did they make a wrong choice against the Lord's will?

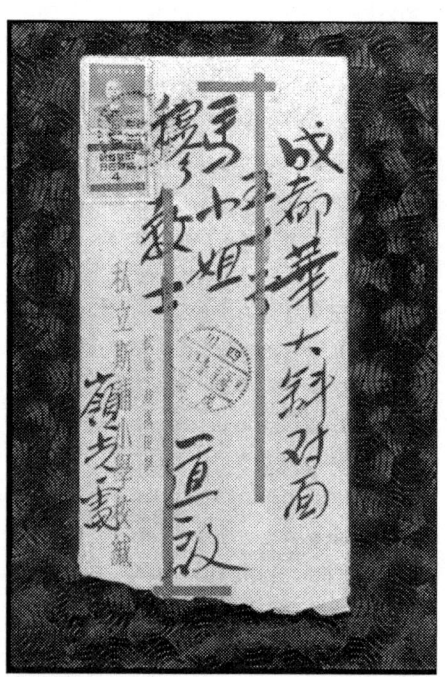

Envelope of the Noso chief's letter
to the girls

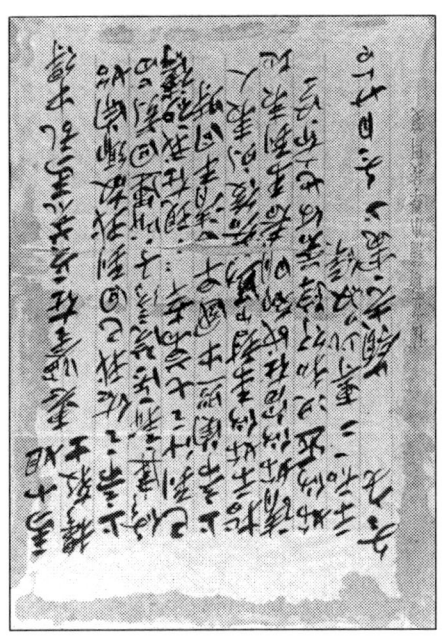

The chief's letter to the girls

Chapter 22
War in Chengdu – 1949

Many Chinese wanted to speak English well enough to pass a test to enter an English speaking country. Helen Jean had such a class of five boys. She taught them Scripture and the meaning of it. Shortly after she started the class she asked one of the boys a question. He just looked at her and said nothing. She asked another the same question. She received the same funny look. She went around the class and found only one boy understood what she was saying. She told him there was no use of her teaching this class. He told her that he walked home with these boys. On the way home he made them understand the meaning of Scripture. He told Helen Jean he had to walk a long ways with them. Before they would reach home they would understand and be able to speak correctly.

The course she used was the Navigators' course. Chinese memorize quickly so the boys soon could say verses which gave them the way of salvation and verses which helped them grow spiritually.

One day in October Helen Jean's language teacher told her she prayed like a child. She just praised the Lord that she even sounded like she was praying. Singing and praying were difficult for Helen Jean for praying involved many words not found in ordinary use. She needed to know the meaning of every word if she were ever going to teach.

By November 12 the girls realized they had no more money. Mail was slow in those days. They could not keep money in the bank for the exchange changed daily. When you received a check you quickly paid your bills before the money was worthless. The girls soon found it wise to buy rice and put it in a footlocker with a lock and key. Each morning the cook would take so much rice to buy the food for the day. Rice became their money. The big silver dollars which the girls once used were outlawed by the government, but rice was not.

On December 9 the girls decided to go shopping down town Chengdu. The streets were full of people who had the same idea. They entered store after store and found them almost completely empty of foods and common household items.

Common medicine was almost impossible to buy. After shopping for some time, they heard a loud noise. People started to run. A truck was coming down the street with a machine gun shooting in all directions. Immediately Louise and Helen Jean found shelter behind a big rock while the machine gun passed by them. Their desire for shopping soon evaporated, and they went home as fast as they could.

On December 12 they took their turn to guard the compound from 9 o'clock to 11 o'clock P.M.

Honey, the Swedish missionary, was a brave one. She did her guarding alone. December 13 was a rough night. Someone fired a rifle. The bullet intended for Honey missed her but struck a tree behind her. The next morning we all knew we were in a real war.

On December 14, Thomas, one of the trusted Chinese asked the girls if they would like to see the battlefield of last night. Helen Jean said, "No, thank you," but Louise wanted to see it. She and Thomas saw many horrible sights. Louise told of the gardener who tried in vain to protect his garden in a bamboo raised platform with a roof. But he was planted in his own garden, bloody and dead.

Roseline, a Hwa Si Ba College student, was the daughter of a minister who had been taken to prison. The congregation prayed for their beloved pastor that somehow he would be released for they needed his wise counsel.

Word came to Roseline's mother to come to the prison and take the cadaver for burial. She got a group from the church and they took the body home. They purchased a big wooden coffin and lined it with grass paper. They put some clean clothes on their beloved pastor and laid his limp body in the coffin. They stood around the coffin crying when someone noticed one of his eyes open. He was not dead, but had suffered a cerebral hemorrhage. God had answered their prayer. He was now out of prison. The last the girls heard of him was that he was preaching again.

News came that the troops were coming to take over Chengdu on December 26, 1949.

Red soldiers took over Chengdu

The marching Red army

Louise and Helen Jean could not understand why some people who were Christians ever planned to go out and welcome them. Fear has great power.

True, there was no money to use. There were no government offices open. The Post Office was out of business. There were no lights nor water, but was this an excuse to welcome an enemy? The very ones who promised to make the country a heaven for them, but could not?

People were desperate and many were dangerous. You went out of your house only when you just had to go for something. Schools and churches were mainly on vacation. The fear of death was on every corner. Many million Chinese were not ready for Satan's wages – death. War is Satan's tool to show his sinful power. Only Christians can overcome war by Christ's resurrection power.

Chapter 23
Food in China 1950

The war left many stores with empty shelves. Very little imported food was found. Only at yard sales of people leaving were canned goods found. At one of these Louise and Helen Jean found two cans of pie cherries which they quickly bought.

The girls were hungry for lettuce. In order to safely eat lettuce it was soaked in a solution which would kill unwanted germs. This did not make the lettuce taste anything like it should.

As a result the girls looked over the area where they lived and decided to have a garden. The closer it was to the house the better it would be. Sometimes garden produce just walked away. They had brought some vegetable seeds from America for just this purpose. Only coolies made gardens but all were willing to be coolies for the lettuce and fresh vegetables they could eat.

Rosalind came over and suggested that some of the students of Hwa Si Ba would be willing to dig the garden for them if the girls would help pay their school fees. They agreed. The garden soon was taking shape. The garden was not extensive, but the girls could see that it was growing and soon they would be enjoying the best lettuce in China.

The girls had an upstairs apartment so they could look down on their garden every morning to see how things had been growing. One morning the apartment seemed to be filled with a terrible smell. They were eating breakfast and decided to check the garden. Below in the garden was the cook's wife carefully doctoring each plant in the garden with "night soil" (human waste)!! Wah! All their hard work was for nothing. Now they could not eat anything from the garden without first cooking it or putting it through that terrible solution.

The cook's wife who fertilized the garden

Salt could not be bought in the store but only from the market. It came in large blocks of dirt and unknown. The cows on Helen Jean's father's farm had better salt than that. The cook would melt it down into a big baking pan and skim off the dirt and unwanted material before he carefully put the baking pan in the oven. The water would evaporate leaving the salt and less debris. Sometimes he would melt it several times before it was white salt. However, the salt became less salty with the number of times it took to evaporate the water. As a result white salt was an expensive item unless you had a cook who would take the time to process it.

Sugar was another item of concern. It came in a big block mainly tan or brown. It was processed like you would make candy. After the sugar was hard it was broken to bits, often looking like lumpy white sand. That is, if they were able to strain out all the undesirable stuff.

This apartment had a big old iron stove with a big oven so it was a good place to process salt and sugar. The Chinese had a big job doing it over a pot of charcoal.

Peanuts were bought in the market in the shell. They had to be roasted, shelled, skinned, and run through the food grinder more than once. By that stage they had really chunky peanut butter. This peanut butter had to be used quickly before the oil came to the top to spoil all that hard work..

Powdered milk was hard to find. The milk on the street was often watered down.

Bread was not a common product to be found. The Chinese used their flour for cakes. When you wanted to bake something you would buy just a cup or two of flour for the need. Flour was not stored in the homes.

On the streets you could find people cooking dough strings. These were fried in deep fat over a pot of charcoal. They tasted something like a donut.

Meat hung in the open. If you wanted some you told them how much to cut. They had no order in cutting the meat, so you might get better or worse cuts of meat depending on progress.

Chickens were sold alive. They were the safest to buy during fly season.

Duck eggs were popular. They had a blue shell and were strong. Chicken eggs often had a chicken in them.

The cook the girls had hired did all the buying of food in the markets and did a good job. How they praised the Lord for him.

When the girls were at Yale they had a Chinese teacher that they dearly loved. She and her husband came to Chengdu. The girls asked Wasa if he could make a pie as they welcomed their guests. That was no problem to him. They had two cans of pie cherries and decided they would see what his piecrust was like.

When the cook served the first pie to the girls the crust was wonderful but there was too much juice with the cherries.

Louise looked up the word for cornstarch and went to the cook and suggested a little cornstarch would make the pie just perfect. He looked at her with a strange look but she repeated it so he seemed to understand for he said, "How la how la".

The day came when Ve Ling came. The cook outdid himself in cooking a wonderful meal. He cleared the table for the desert, brought on the dishes, pie and knife.

Ve Ling was our guest so he set the pie in front of her. She admired it greatly. She took up the knife to cut each of us a piece but had a very difficult time going through the top crust. She lifted up little piece and found sliced whole ginger under the top crust. Louise's use of the word with the wrong tone had made cornstarch into whole ginger. Ve Ling laughed, pulled out the ginger and they ate the nippy cherry pie. The cook had known enough to thicken the juice so all went well.

The use of the wrong tone has kept most of the missionaries humble.

Chapter 24
Uncertain Days in 1950

The China Inland Mission had a good-sized compound and church in Chengdu. This was in the main a Baptist area. However, as the war progressed missionaries from out stations came to Chengdu for protection.

Born again Christians met together for prayer. Louise and Helen Jean went across town weekly to the prayer meeting. From week to week none of them knew who would be missing the next prayer meeting or why.

Each week a different missionary led devotions. On June 3 Helen Jean was asked to lead. She chose Daniel 6:10 because of Daniel's encouraging example of praying despite political pressure to ignore God in his daily life. Wah! That would deny our very reason for being in China!

On the way to prayer meeting she had to bike through deep water because of the rain. She ran over something in the dark that caused her bike to tip over and dump her into some very dirty water. She was near the Knights' missionary home and stopped to see if she could get some dry clothes.

This caused her to be a bit late. She did not know what the missionaries had said before she arrived. Later she found out they had decided that they must change their style of work so that the government would not stop them. When Helen Jean read how Daniel prayed before an open window as he had done in the past the whole gang was challenged to forget about changing their style of work.

What a prayer meeting they had. There was confession of sin, determination to trust the Lord to work through the tough times. God helped Daniel; He would help them no matter what happened.

Then on January 4, 1950, Miss Syau was found dead. She was from a poor home, a student who had become a soldier for the old Chinese government to earn money for her schooling. She was found gagged, beaten over the top of her head, and dumped into an open grave. They had some evidence that assured them that she is with the Lord. She came to the services in their big living room. Only the true Christians ever dared to come.

Only the day before that tragic discovery, Mr. Phillips, the overseer of the area where the girls lived, announced they would have to move. The new president of Hwa Si Ba wanted to live in their house. This meant they would have to move. "Where?" was the $64 question. How much it would cost was another problem. It was an unsettling time.

Later that week a huge truck barely missed Helen Jean's bike on a crowded street. There must have been an angel that kept it from crushing her or the bike. The Lord still had more work for her to do.

Every household had a cook who bought food for those for whom he worked. The new government insisted all cooks meet with them on January 10. They all had to be brainwashed. Wasa, the girls' cook, was a Christian and did not fall for their thinking.

In spite of all this unrest the weekend meeting saw twenty-two students meet in their living room to pray, sing, and learn more of what the Bible said.

February 4, 1950, was a marked day for Helen Jean. This was the first time she ever prayed in Chinese in public. Oh, she had prayed in Chinese in small groups and for her teachers but never in a large group. Just singing in Chinese from the hymnbook was difficult enough. By the grace of God she learned both to sing and to pray.

On February 13 instead of receiving a handful of valentines, Helen Jean was given a pile of Christmas cards from the mail. Never mind, she savored each one, and just thinking of how they thought of her at Christmas was a blessing to her.

February 20 Emily, a Chinese student at Hwa Si Ba, told Helen Jean about her life as a young person. She had grown up in an unbelieving home and as a child had gone to school in the temple. Helen Jean asked her if the temple was still like it was when she went to school. She assured her it was. The temple was not too far away and they could bike there in a short while. When they arrived a soldier was in the gatehouse with a gun, not the usual man Emily had known. She asked if they could take pictures for Helen Jean hoped to make a child's book of Emily's life. He granted permission and they proceeded to the temple. What they did not know was that the soldiers had taken over the temple. When they started to take pictures three soldiers ordered them to stop. They asked them to take their bikes to the police station for such an offence. This meant one soldier with a gun in front of them leading the way and two behind to see that they went in the right direction. The temple was a long trip on foot rolling their bike to the main police station.

Emily (on right) and friend,
Emily raised in temple schools

When they arrived Emily told the police about the situation but the story of the three soldiers was a bit different. They took Helen Jean's camera and told the girls to wait on a hard wooden bench. After hours of waiting they had taken the film and gave Helen Jean back her camera, now broken. They were now free to go home on their bikes.

In the meantime someone had seen Emily, Helen Jean and the soldiers. They immediately went to tell Louise. Praise God, He answers prayer. Somehow the desire to write a children's book about Emily evaporated.

Every day, Louise and Helen Jean were teaching classes, studying and helping students spiritually. Daily, people were guests at their table. War days are hard on all people.

Chapter 25
Student Work 1950

Louise and Helen Jean's apartment was like Grand Central Station from the time they got up in the morning until they retired at night. They had no radio or TV but news came in spurts by word of mouth.

After the take over on April 29, the students of Hwa Si Ba were put into little groups. They had to encourage one another to be good Communists. No more than one Christian was put in each of these small groups so that more pressure was brought on them.

However, at Chwan Daw University on August 23, when they made up the small groups all the Christians were put in one group.

In Louise and Helen Jean's student meetings, Christians who had had a rough time were encouraged by Christians who had victory over some difficult situation. Their testimony meetings gave insight of what was happening. After the testimony each time a clear Bible message helped to strengthen the believers.

On the streets any time of the day you could hear children, or young people or adults practicing a song and dance which seem to united the Red Party and their work. The song had a catchy tune so it became very popular. The dance seemed to go with it.

On June 27th news came to the girls that General Douglas McArthur was sent for the purpose of fighting in the Far East. As a result of this, on June 29th the Sunday school on 12th Street was closed.

The girls continued to study the Chinese Bible each available hour and work with students.

When July 14th came the students had very little money but they wanted to do something for Helen Jean's birthday. They pooled their money and got a little cake with Chinese characters saying "Happy Birthday". If it had been for a Chinese they would have the message in English. They knew the Chinese characters would mean more to Helen Jean.

On July 19th a missionary from another mission informed the girls they must leave when he left. He was fearful and left shortly afterwards. The girls didn't feel their work was completed or that the Lord wanted them to leave, yet.

At the testimony time of the July 27th students' meeting Lyou We Hawei challenged the whole group. Her school had to be brainwashed so the students of the school were taken to a large field. The student body sat on the grass with the fierce summer sun beating down on them. The weather was super hot in that field. Lyou We Hawei felt she was going to faint. She prayed to the Lord to send a breeze or to cool the place somehow. After she prayed, a big Chinese fellow in front of her stood up and cast a comforting shadow on her. Jeremiah 33:3 became real.

At the time of the takeover and during these brainwashing days, grass shoes and well-worn clothes were in style. Both Louise and Helen Jean wore Chinese blue gowns but not grass shoes. They were considered wealthy because each of them had a bike. No one knew all the headaches they had with the bikes.

Medical work was always present. Mrs. Blossner, a missionary nurse, lived in an apartment downstairs from where the girls lived. She was going to have a baby but started to run a fever of 104 degrees. As a nurse she knew it had to come down. Helen Jean went to help her. None of the medicine the girls had could be used because of complications. Helen Jean then started to bathe her with cool water and forced fluids that were cool. After a couple of hours she checked her temperature and found it was back down to 101.4 degrees. She felt safe to release Helen Jean from caring for her. By the next morning the fever had left her.

Around that same time the cook's little boy was yellow. He was a very sick little boy but the cook's wife insisted on taking him to a witch to help him.

Mrs. Bright told us about a poor lady who was walking along the street and felt she was going to have a baby. She immediately slipped into a smelly outside street toilet and there delivered her own baby. According to her culture she could not leave the place of delivery for one month. How she and the baby lived through that August is a great wonder.

On August 1st a shower of pink slips were dropped from a plane, directing all foreigners to go home. Within two days the radio brought news that eight million people who were not doing as the new government "suggested" had been killed.

In spite of all this the girls kept studying their Chinese Bibles and working with students who came to them for help.

Chapter 26
The Move Is On

Missionaries Rev. and Mrs. Knight had a baby girl. They had to buy milk for her. When they noticed that the baby's legs were abnormal, they took her to the doctor and he told them she had rickets. She desperately needed milk. They had been buying milk on the street. Then they discovered that milk had been replaced by water and something that made it look like milk.

The girls realized if they left China the Christians might be fed with a watered down Bible so they encouraged the students to memorize the Scripture verses put out by the Navigators. At that time they were in contact with several colleges. The students would come to the girls and say their verses and pick up a new set of verses. The art school students came and made Helen Jean some lovely backgrounds for the flannel graph board. They did a super job on the manger scene. It looks like a dirty barn. One such background arrived on August 20.

On August 21st six new students started their memory work.

In January of 1950 the girls had been told that the president of Hwa Si Ba University wanted their flat. They would have to move. In August this became a reality for the girls. The students went house hunting for them. It was difficult for an American to find a house and to decide on how much rent should be paid.

After many days they found places but none seemed to fit the range of Helen Jean and Louise's meager income. They were presumed to be rich foreigners.

On September 5 a home was found outside the city wall. The owner wanted to live in part of the house. It had a wall around the building and its small yard. It also had a fairly large living room. In the back of the house were two kitchens that went with the house. Behind the house and wall many poor people eked out a living. About a yard away from the dining room window was the neighbor's barn. If the window was open the unwanted farm odors filled the dining room.

In spite of the way the house was situated, this seemed to be the only house which the girls could afford. Roseland hired for them a log wagon pulled by four or six men and eleven rickshaws to move the girl's belongings to the new house. The girls cleaned each room, closet, hall and kitchens. Louise had bought a little laundry stove for a house they thought was going to be their home but something happened so they rented the one they less desired.

Both of the kitchens in back of the house had some kind of stove so Louise's stove stood on the porch. It would not look good in the bedroom, dining room or living room. The weather in Chengdu is cloudy most of the time so leather goods and metals suffer. Shoes are sunned and cleaned about anytime there was a sun shining. Metals are oiled to keep the rust off. Only the Lord could solve the problem of what to do with the stove.

On September 11 Louise decided to houseclean the clothes closet top, sides and floor. While she was cleaning the walls, they seem to move. She called Helen Jean. They found a secret panel. The back of the closet fell open to a storage space.

In it were many lovely China vases, which had Chinese characters on them. The girls learned later these were given to the owner's husband for being a hero in the old Chinese army. The girls moved the vases carefully and measured the space left. They then went to the stove on the porch and did some measuring.

Wah! It was a perfect fit for the space. Carefully they pulled and pushed the little stove into the space. The wall of the closet went back in place. Only the girls knew what happened to the stove when it disappeared.

On September 21 the police banged at the gate of the outer wall. They heard the girls had barrels of gasoline. They had a warrant to search the house. They came in three different times and found nothing. What they did not know was that Louise had two or three fruit jars of cleaning fluid (which really was high octane gasoline) in a footlocker. They however, were looking for big barrels which the girls did not have.

On September 30 Emily finished a lovely blue wool sweater for Helen Jean. It was a real blessing to Helen Jean since there was no heat in the house which remained chilly through the long winter.

Often at night there came a sound like a cat on the roof of the house. The girls were unaware that robbers called to one another from roof to roof with cat sounds. Louise got a pail of water and threw it at what sounded like a cat. That was the end of catcalls.

As that October began a missionary who had been working in a college some miles away decided to move close to Hwa Si Ba where the girls did most of their work. Due to that travel distance, fewer and fewer students were coming outside the campus to their place. The girls were not discouraged for right behind their house was a mission field. Working with students was far different than working with the poor.

Rosaland helped the girls to empty their living room of all available furniture before any of the meetings. Often at the ladies meetings little children came with their mothers. The girls' living room floor became the bathroom for those visiting children.

Their living room was often filled with children for Sunday school. These children lived behind their wall and came to them from the back gate.

They also found there were many ladies in this area who could not read. The China Inland Mission had paperback books which taught people to read as well as to teach them how to become a Christian. The girls purchased a number of these books. Soon you could hear the ladies read, "I am a sinner. You are a sinner. We all are sinners." in Chinese.

A teen-age boy who could not read asked if he could join the ladies. He soon could read well.

For them to understand that Christ died for them was not too difficult for they often killed a chicken to appease their paper gods. They needed to shift their gaze to the Lamb of God.

These books were not only a help to those who could not read but helped the girls to be able to give the gospel in simple words to the unsaved.

On October 14 the police delivered an ultimatum: the girls had only six more months to live in China.

On October 15 some letters finally came from America. One came from Baptist Mid-Missions, the first one in four long months.

The girls were happy in their new home. After they had finished a complete housecleaning job, adding curtains to the windows and a few pictures to the walls, they were satisfied. They continued to work on the language when they were not in meetings with ladies or children or students. This serenity could not last for long.

Chapter 27
Last Days in China

The girls had been given only six more months to live in China. They tried to make the most of every day for the Lord. The new government under Communist leadership was not going to tolerate foreign teachers who disagreed with their beliefs and methods.

They were reaching the children behind their house in Bible clubs. The university students were helping them so a number were introduced to the Lord.

The ladies behind their house were coming to reading classes. Their very own books were telling them the gospel as they struggled to read each page.

Students from several colleges were learning verses from the Navigators course, which helped them grow spiritually.

The girls found a little printing shop that had translated many Christian books. They bought as many as they could. They set up a library for the students who came to say their verses. Books went out as soon as they were returned if they were good. The library looked like a partly empty bookcase most of the time.

By November 24 they were able to get 92 more good books. One of the students who was a good preacher fell heir to this library when the girls had to leave it behind.

The girls treated many of the people behind their house. Pink eye was a common ailment. Soon it was known these girls could help them when they were sick. In November a Chinese lady with a huge sore came to see the girls. It was so big it looked like a mountain with a core at the top. The girls asked who her doctor was, and she told them. They told her to go to him and get a paper with permission for the girls to try a shot of penicillin. Helen Jean had saved a bottle with one mold, which was used to prepare the penicillin in case either she or Louise was very sick. At that time she would activate the mold with a solution. From the looks of things the girls would not need to use it on themselves. The lady needed it now or she would die. When she came back with a note from the doctor Helen Jean gave her the shot. Six weeks later she came back to see the girls. The sore had healed nicely. She felt much better, praise the Lord.

On November 14, Mr. Pan, their teacher, came to them fearful to tell them he could not teach them anymore. They should find another teacher.

Almost every week someone was borrowing flannelgraph figures for stories they wanted to teach to some class of children in the city.

November 16 was a sad day as the students informed the girls that their cook's baby had died. They asked about the funeral but the student responded, "Oh, they just rolled him up in a mat of straw and put him in the garbage!" Jesus did not think of life as so cheap.

The situation was deteriorating steadily. On December 2 the girls were told they were not needed in the student work anymore. Three days later the warnings became a little stronger that they should stay home from the students' meetings. By the end of that week the girls were told by a foreigner to just go home. The girls ceased going places at night. To stay home was much safer. During the day if they saw papers falling from a plane or people marching and shouting about the evils of foreigners they also stayed home.

During the winter in Chengdu the weather is chilly. No heat is found in the houses. Many of the people have red raised spots on their hands and feet. They call these "dung burs" which are chilblains, not at all comfortable. Many of the people wear gloves with part of the fingers exposed so they can write and work.

In mid-December Mr. Vinden, a dear old man from England who had spent his life in China as a missionary, seriously warned the girls to leave. He confessed that he and his family had applied to leave long ago but were hindered. There were too many Chinese who spoke against him and his wife. Maybe that would be their lot too. So the girls found their way to the Foreign Affairs Office on December 19th, depending on the Lord for guidance as to what to do. Soon afterward people were on the street yelling at the foreigners that they should leave their country.

The girls had been told if they wanted to save their pictures they should pull them out of their photo albums and send the pictures to Hong Kong where they had some of their things stored to take home. Now what does one do with an empty photo album? Helen Jean found in one of her footlockers some Sunday school papers for beginners with pictures of the Life of Christ on the front covers. She found enough to tell the complete story of Christ. She pasted them in the empty photo album. She then placed the album on the coffee table in the living room. Someone would value the story of Jesus.

On December 20 Mr. Yau arrived with many questions. Rosland informed the girls he had turned and was working for the new government. Helen Jean answered his questions but he left in a rage. In the meantime people started to pray for him. At year's end he came back to see Helen Jean but saw the photo album on the coffee table. She asked him if he would like to see some pictures. He was so willing he sat down as Helen Jean opened the album and explained as she went along. He was very quiet. At the end he said, "Isn't there another way to heaven?" and left. He had memorized Scripture. He had seen the way of life that Christ had provided for him but the girls never knew if he became a Christian or not. To be become a Christian would mean he would have to leave the party but he wanted the money.

When the girls went to church they were not welcome anymore. People were afraid to be seen talking to them. Going to and from church was always dangerous. Only the fearless few of the students came to their house now to say verses, to borrow books, or just to visit. They actually endangered the students by being associated with them.

The ladies went back home and found that their little walled house had been sold out from under them. They would have to move. The closure of the deal was December 25th. Some Merry Christmas that was! On December 31 the girls were informed that they could remain in the house until they left town. The very next day they celebrated the New Year by telling the students they were leaving China. The students told them that they had known it for some time. Diary entries relate the sad story as 1951 got underway.

January 4 – Some of the missionary children who were home for Christmas vacation came to see Louise and Helen Jean. The girls realized they could only take a little bit of luggage home so they asked the girls if they would like some of their wardrobe. Oh! They were so happy to have some new clothes in their style.

January 5 – Papers came to be filled out. Louise and Helen Jean, fearful they might write the wrong Chinese characters, got their teacher to fill out the papers for them. Pastor Dunn was happy to do this for them. No one received their exit papers as quickly as those girls did!

The girls gave away things people could use without getting into trouble with the new government. The benches they had used for the student work they gave to the leaders of the students to be passed down to be used in their work for the Lord. The left over medicine they gave to nurses who were eager to get it.

January 13 – Helen Jean sold her bike and signed over her papers to the buyer.

Helen Jean's precious bike in Chengdu

January 15 – Louise sold her bike. Each of them now had some local money for a bus trip to Chungking.

They had two great problems. The first was to get a storekeeper to sign for them to guarantee they had good character and would not cause the new government any trouble. They knew no storekeepers since their servant did most of the buying. However, they had bought many books from a print shop and the owner was willing to sign for them.

The next difficult step was to go to the bank saying they had no other money but the local money. Helen Jean had one silver dollar but Louise had a gold bar so on January 12 Louise went to the bank. They took the money, gave Louise a receipt and said they would keep her money safe. And they did keep it safe from her – they just kept it!

January 14 – This was the last night they would be in their little rented house. They invited all the children and people behind the house to come and see slides of the Life of Christ. The place was jammed.

The slides started and one little boy got up and ran out of the building through the back gate. Very shortly he came with his little sister and had her sit down close to him. In a few minutes he was gone again. This time he brought another person and explained a bit of the exciting events he had seen.

Often when Helen Jean thinks of that little boy she cannot help hoping she might be as interested in others to bring them to the place they can come to know the Lord.

The numerous subtle signals added up to one clear message: they would have to leave China quite soon. To remain there would endanger the Chinese brothers and sisters who would seek to protect them. They had enough trouble coping with their own families' needs without the added work and hazards of hiding foreigners. Once this difficult decision was made, the complicated process of leaving China was finally underway. They had faithfully followed God's calling to China, but their course there was now complete.

Chapter 28
Leaving China

After showing the slides of the Life of Christ to a house full of poor people who lived behind Louise and Helen Jean's rented home, they slept one more night before they left Chengdu. The morning came too fast. Quickly two rickshaws were obtained. Good byes were said, luggage loaded and each of them was buried under it. Each had a thermos of water and a confirmed bus ticket to Chungking. Lord willing, they would stay over night in Chungking at the China Inland Mission station and get a ship that would take them down the Yangtze River the next day.

The girls' rented home was outside the city wall. In order to get to the bus station they would have to go through the gate of the wall. The police saw two foreigners coming with much luggage. Their only thought was these two girls have things to conquer Chengdu. With that in mind they searched them carefully. The girls showed them their bus tickets but that didn't change their minds about really searching them. They found nothing threatening so let them proceed to the bus station under careful watch.

After the girls arrived in the city, every block where a police was directing traffic the girls were searched. One of the police even looked in each of their thermos bottles but only found water. The many searches took time. January 15, 1951, dragged on and on, the longest day of their lives.

When they arrived at the bus station the bus was about to leave. The girls showed them their confirmed tickets but they said there was only space for one of them to ride the bus. Their confirmed tickets were for seats in the middle of the bus and a man had taken one of the seats. The bus driver had made money on this man's ticket so did not want to refund it. Then the driver informed the girls that one of them could sit up in front with him. They said, "No, we have confirmed tickets and we are to sit in the middle of the bus together." Why the middle of the bus? Foreigners would not be noticed for searching mixed in with the local people. At last the man who was sitting in one of their seats said he would sit up with the driver. The girls praised the Lord that they had their seats together.

Chinese buses are made for people smaller than Americans. The roads are not smooth so the girls could take their choice as they went over bumps – skin off their knees or skin off their backs. All day the girls traveled and were looking forward to a good bed, supper, and band aids for their knees and backs.

When they arrived at the China Inland Mission station they were shocked by the welcome company. There were about forty-four people waiting for a ship and none was available. The mission did make a place for the girls. The next morning the girls were asked if they would like to help teach the children who were with their parents at the mission. Many of the children had missed many days of school while traveling. Helen Jean had taught elementary grades 1 through 8 so knew what should be taught and was willing to help.

Each day the men who were living at the mission went to the river to see if a ship had arrived. Chinese New Years came and no one wanted to travel down the river. Immediately news came, "Ship available."

The men went to buy tickets and were able to get forty-six tickets, one for each who wanted to leave Chungking. Not all of the people who stayed at the China Inland Mission station were missionaries; some were embassy people, a good number were children with parents. One of the embassy men felt it wise to send his wife and baby with a group of missionaries so she and the baby were among the welcome group.

The ship was going down to the city of Wanshen. Helen Jean was searched and the police found her diary. They took her to a room where a group of police were seated. Each was given a few pages of her diary to read. They all read with one eye on the sheets and one on her. They found nothing of political subversion. The leader collected the sheets and gave then back to Helen Jean. After she got on the ship she tore up the sheets of the diary and dumped them into the Yangtse River. She did not want this to happen again or for her to be put in prison for some misunderstanding. What a loss that was! But the pages were written in her heart and have now been recorded for posterity.

Because there were so many foreigners some of them were on fifth class which was on the open deck on the third deck of the ship. This meant their space was on the floor of the deck where people walked from one cabin to the next. The girls rolled out their bedrolls on a piece of "yo bu" (Chinese oilcloth) and tried to keep warm as they looked at the lovely sights as they went by. Sometimes the rocks looked like thinly sliced bread, other times the rocks were pink or lovely green or wine colored. They were sights they would never forget.

Before Helen Jean left Chengdu many people suggested she sell her fur coat which her father had given her when she was in Bible School. Helen Jean felt otherwise and got a Chinese tailor to make her a gown she could wear over her coat. The gown looked much like what the Chinese would wear. While on the third deck for a day and night the air became more than chilly. Helen Jean praised the Lord He directed her to keep her nice warm coat for no breeze seemed to penetrate it. Her coat kept her from getting a terrible cold.

When the ship arrived in Wanshan the police escorted them to a place much like a prison. However, the men were able to get fifth class tickets for the forty-six of them to Ichang.

The ship had docked in the harbor away from the dock. In order to get on this ship they had to walk across little boats to their ship. One of the ladies had three children. She was fearful one of them would miss a boat so Louise and Helen Jean each took one child to help them to the ship. The mother took the youngest.

When they arrived on the ship the men told them they would be on the lower deck with the coal and cargo. They should take up as much space as possible on the floor of the ship. All the ladies went to work to save space on the floor. Helen Jean had a long space.

The hatch was closed and the men came to find their wives. Helen Jean's space was beside the wife of one of the missionaries. She told Helen Jean her husband had helped get Helen Jean's luggage on the ship. Now he had no place to lie down. There was a smaller space not too far away. Would she like to go there and give him her long space? Helen Jean was not too happy to do so but her luggage was safe because of him so she gave up her space. The smaller space was around the pole with a funny chain attached. Very quickly she found that this chain was attached to the anchor. Every time it was pulled up it dripped water on whoever was near. Immediately the men put up some Chinese oilcloth and ran it into a wash pan. When the pan got full they emptied it.

Helen Jean was really feeling sorry for herself until she learned that the next morning the Chinese lady who saved the space next to her long space was picking off lice and tossing them over on the place she would have had. Helen Jean was thankful for a few drops of water instead of a population of lice.

Everyone was happy when they arrived in Hankau. The police escorted them to a lovely hotel. All forty-six needed a bath. The coal and cargo had changed the color of their skin. The next day they met in a lobby where they looked one another over. They had fun checking over the places each had missed when they took a bath. Some had coal marks on their neck, others on their ears. Some even could stand to return to the bathroom to clean off coal dust. What a wonderful thing to have a bathroom. However, with forty-six it was really an overworked place!

After being inspected by the police the men of the group went to buy tickets for the train to Hong Kong. They were able to get compartment tickets. Louise and Helen Jean were put with Mr. and Mrs. York.

They arrived in Canton, China, where they were told the money they were using was of no value in Hong Kong. So Louise and Helen Jean went shopping and were able to buy many useful things. Sad to say when they arrived in Hong Kong this was just a rumor about the money. Nevertheless, they put to use the things they bought.

The group was able to take a train within about a mile of the border. Everyone had to get out and walk to the border. Coolies carried their luggage to the border.

When Louise and Helen Jean arrived at the border the sun was going down. They could not help thinking the sun was going down on any work they could ever do in China again. So many people going to hell! So few to tell them about Jesus. Many would never hear how He made a way for them to go to Heaven by dying for their sin. To leave China was far more soul wrenching for both of them than going there in the first place.

Chapter 29
Give Up Being a Missionary? No!

God had called Helen Jean to China. There was do doubt in her mind about this but now what was she to do? She was not alone in this problem. Hong Kong was full of missionaries coming out of China with the same question in mind.

Some missionaries who had been called to China under Baptist Mid-Missions started a work in Japan when they found they could no longer go to China. The culture in Japan was entirely different. Only the Kanji character writing of China was similar to that of the people in Japan.

While in Bible School Helen Jean had had a real burden for Ceylon, an island off the coast of India now known as Sri Lanka. Did the Lord want her to go there? She went to the consulate for India and applied. Visas to India took time. This was something Helen Jean did not know.

Louise felt led to go to Japan and left. Others were leaving for other parts of the world but what about Helen Jean? Weariness seemed to be her lot. To go where the Lord led her and when He wanted her there was a real problem. Ships and planes were booked full. To go anywhere in the world meant waiting for some time.

When Helen Jean decided to go back to America she had peace. She was immediately booked on a French ship going to France. On board ship she met a French schoolteacher who had taught French in a public school. Helen Jean asked her to teach her French when there were no sights to see and in turn, she would teach her English.

Neither one of them learned too much but it made their tired minds productive.

The captain announced a special dinner. They could wear costumes if they liked. Helen Jean had bought some thimble-like silver buttons and wondered how she could use them. She had some black ribbon and made boards for her shoulders on a baby blue suit of hers. She put a button on each board and then put the rest of the buttons down the front of her suit. From a quick look you would think Helen Jean was a captain in the Air Force. The only thing she lacked was a captain's hat. The captain saw her and wanted to deport her at the first port near there. She assured him it was only a costume, which he had desired.

When they came to Djibouti the weather was so hot she stayed on board ship. Others got off and told her about the city and brought her pictures. They had their choice to go through the Suez Canal or go see the pyramids. Because of the heat she chose to go through the canal. What an experience! On the other side of the canal they picked up the people who went to see the pyramids.

They sailed through the Mediterranean Sea and landed in France. Helen Jean took a train to visit workers with Baptist Mid-Missions in Paris. Dan and Ida Feryance wanted her to help them in Europe but she did not feel led to do so. After a few days she was booked on the "America" to land in New York.

After arriving in America Helen Jean had meetings back-to-back for about a year. At times she had several meetings in a week. She depended on the meeting in which she spoke to give her enough money to get to the next meeting. Since she did not have a car most of her traveling was done on the Greyhound bus. She sat near the front of the bus close to the door so she did not have to endure the smoke on the bus. She often laughed when arriving at a meeting and would tell the people she had "bus cologne" on today.

The Lord blessed in meetings but this was not working with Chinese. Mr. Arthur Fetzer, who was then the Foreign Secretary in the home office, suggested she go and help Pastor Loong who was working with Chinese in Indonesia. He was a missionary under Baptist Mid-Missions and had gone to America for his schooling. His wife and children had come out of southern China and gone to Indonesia where Pastor Loong's sister and husband lived. His brother-in-law was a wealthy man who made furniture. Pastor Loong had a house church going but not organized yet. They needed help, would she go? This work was in the city of Djakarta, on the island of Java. Pastor Loong spoke Cantonese, English and Mandarin, but preached in Mandarin and it was interpreted into Hakka.

If Helen Jean would go there she would need to go to Yale University for eleven weeks in the summer when they offered instruction in the Indonesian Language. Was this the Lord's will?

She went to help her brother who lived on a farm and had a sick wife. One day as she was having devotions a Scripture verse popped out at her. "Why sit we here until we die?" II Kings 7:3 She told her brother she had to go to Yale for the summer and learn Indonesian. Again Helen's folks could not understand her choice.

Chapter 30
Off to Indonesia

Going to Yale University to study is a big undertaking. Helen Jean found many brilliant people in her Indonesian class. The US Government sent some there. Others were there to write books of diplomatic importance. Helen Jean felt like a dummy among these brilliant men. However, the day arrived when she finished her Indonesian classes with a passing grade.

In the meantime Jane was accepted for Indonesia by Baptist Mid-Missions. Jane and Helen Jean applied for their visas. On September 30, 1954, Mr. Fetzer called Helen Jean to inform her that her visa had arrived but Jane's was rejected.

To wait for a new application for Indonesia might mean years. Mr. Fetzer was willing that she go alone in view of her experience. Helen Jean sent her luggage to the Home of Peace, a place on the West Coast that helps missionaries going overseas.

November 29, 1954, she and her luggage were taken to the "Steel King" ship. This was a large freighter going to Djakarta where she hoped to serve the Lord. There were about ten passengers going different places along the route. Freighters are slow-going ships which stop many places along the way to unload cargo of different types.

On a passenger ship you seldom see the captain, but on this freighter the captain and officers ate in the same dining room and at the same time as the passengers. Thanksgiving was spent on the ship without family and friends but the ship's galley served up a festive meal typical of an American Thanksgiving dinner.

Christmas would also come and go before the ship arrived at her destination. The captain asked the passengers to decorate the dining room for him. Helen Jean had some lovely backgrounds and flannel graph figures so she put them up on one wall of the dining room. They really told the story of Christmas but the captain came in to inspect the decorating and decided that was <u>too</u> much Christmas! All the flannelgraph had to be taken down. Later someone put up decorations which just gave "Season's Greetings."

At long last the day arrived when the ship docked in Djakarta, Indonesia. Pastor Loong and some of the men of the church helped Helen Jean off the ship with her footlockers and luggage. She was taken to a house on Djalan Gedong in which she had two private rooms and also a private bathroom. This seemed like luxury after her accommodations in China! There was a kitchen out back that she shared with others living in the house. In the other part of the house were workers' quarters for those who worked for Mr. Jyung in his factory. During the day they were making leather luggage and purses. At night they came home to their rooms to relax and listen to wild music. Helen Jean wondered how long she could stand this noise at night but she had to be thankful she was in a place where they needed the gospel.

The church was meeting in the home of Mrs. Lee from Sumatra. She owned a tin mine and often had to come to Djakarta so had purchased this house. She told Pastor Loong he could use the house for a church Sundays and during the week. It had a huge living room connected with a good-sized dining room. The church had its own chairs. After each meeting the chairs were stacked so Mrs. Lee could use her building if she had need of it.

Pastor Loong had asked Helen Jean to bring a communion set for the church. Until that time they had used open salt shakers for communion cups on a tray. Mrs. Loong bought raisins and boiled them. The water became the grape juice they used for communion. Mrs. Loong made the bread in a fry pan with oil and flour. The bread looked like a big round pancake. When the bread came to you, you pulled a piece off, which might stretch two or three inches before you got a piece.

Pastor Loong was a man's man. He had a wonderful way with men. The church was full of men. Mrs. Loong played the piano for singing and one or two other women were brave enough to come to church. The first Sunday Helen Jean was in church she sat with one other lady. After the service Pastor Loong asked Helen Jean to go to the door and he would introduce her to the people.

Pastor Ernest Loong and family

One after another was introduced. Most of the men were built like high school students. To her surprise they were married men with several children. Of the whole group that Sunday only two boys turned out to be young people.

Outside the house children played. Helen Jean asked why they didn't sit inside and listen? Was there no Sunday school? Pastor Loong assured her that was her new job. She asked about the Young Peoples' group. That too was her job. "Where were the ladies?" was the next question. Well, that would be her job too!

Pastor Loong had what he called Young Peoples but he announced Helen Jean would take charge of it. January 7th of 1955 was her first Young Peoples meeting. She expected just the two boys but a whole group of married men came. She told them Young Peoples meant only unmarried people.

This did not make the men happy but the two boys enjoyed it. They went calling on their friends and soon there was a good group of unsaved teenaged girls and boys who were coming.

The two boys were saved and loved the Lord so they were a big help to Helen Jean. Today Swei Loong, one of the boys, is a senior pastor here in America in a Chinese Church with a very large congregation. The other boy, Tung Hwa, is in Taiwan. Helen Jean has not heard what has become of him.

Swei Loong who later became a pastor

On January 23rd the Sunday school began. Helen Jean had gone to language school for Indonesian and Chinese but could neither pray nor sing well in the languages. One of the men of the church, Mr. Chen Mu Lin, could speak Keh Hwa and Indonesian but did not speak Mandarin. He helped Helen Jean with the Sunday school.

At first there were mostly grade school children who came. The adults were not interested in Sunday school. Despite all the difficulties of that first year they enjoyed an average attendance of sixty-seven students.

February 4th was the first meeting of the ladies. The ladies' work was the most difficult work Helen Jean had. They spoke Keh Hwa, Cantonese, Mandarin, Indonesia and another dialect from Southern China. Helen Jean would give a short devotion and then ask for prayer requests. The ladies liked to kneel when praying. Each lady was given a pillow with a print pillowcase to kneel in comfort. They also used these pillows during the week at the church's prayer meeting. One of the ladies saw to it that the pillowslips were clean and ironed by a charcoal iron.

Ladies calling for the church

Mrs. Jyung did not see any sense in Helen Jean's work and made it known. Pastor Loong suggested Helen Jean give her a gift and talk to her. Wah! A wealthy lady, what could she give? Pastor Loong suggested a special duck. He knew she liked this meat. Helen Jean took the little money she had to buy a duck. She followed the directions Pastor Loong gave and soon recognized the place.

She brought the duck to the Jyung's home. She knocked at the door and the servant came. She told Helen Jean that Mrs. Jyung was sleeping. She gave the duck to the servant and left. Mrs. Jyung awoke and the servant told her about the duck. She was angry. She let it be known she did not like that American.

Pastor Loong realized he would have to do something about Mrs. Jyung. He told his wife he would fast and pray for Mrs. Jyung. Mrs.

Jyung loved to gamble with dominos, which they called mahjong. She had strong influence over all the ladies. After several days of fasting and praying he wrote Mrs. Jyung a letter. Wei Nai, pastor Loong's son delivered the letter to her. She was enraged. Wei Nai left and after getting home told his father what happened. Pastor Loong went on fasting and praying.

Mrs. Jyung decided to go see Pastor Loong to tell him off. When she arrived Wei Nai met her and asked her if she would like some tea. No, she wanted to see Pastor Loong. Wei Nai gave her a chair but she wasn't about to sit. Wei Nai went to Pastor Loong's study and announced Mrs. Jyung was in the living room waiting to see him.

He came out pale, thin, and tired looking from praying and fasting. Immediately she knew why he looked so weakened. She confessed her sin and got right with the Lord.

Later all could see she wanted to follow the Lord for she offered her car and chauffeur to go calling on the ladies to invite them to come to church. Helen Jean and Mrs. Jyung were often seen calling on ladies together. As a result the ladies' work grew to about fifty people.

Chapter 31
Struggles Faced in Indonesia

Shortly after Helen Jean arrived in Indonesia her two little rooms seemed too hot and uncomfortable. She went to the table where she would eat her dinner and wondered if she could endure this heat.

The servant that she was given was called Si. Si announced in Indonesian that someone had brought her a present. It was a big pear-shaped citrus fruit. Si told her to try it. She might like it. Helen Jean sat at the table peeling this huge fruit. She found the flavor was much like a grapefruit. The more she ate the more she wanted. Very soon the uncomfortable hot feeling left her. Wah! She could eat one of these and be comfortable. She could live in the tropics! The season for the fruit lasted for some time. When there was no more pamalo she wondered what would happen. She was visiting in a home and the lady of the house introduced her to limes. One lime, if large, could make two glasses of limeade. This seemed to take the place of pamalo. Limes seemed to be available every season. Only the Lord could provide so well.

Pastor and Mrs. Loong were concerned about Helen Jean that she would not get overheated so they picked her up in their car to go to church. The day arrived when the tropics did not seem to bother Helen Jean. Pastor Loong suggested she learn to drive on the opposite side of the road than we Americans use. She passed the driving test but her support would never be able to pay for a car, much less keep it going.

She decided to get a bicycle. When the church heard about this they offered to pay for it. A group went to the bike shop and they picked out a green one for her. It proved to be a good one. From then on when she wanted to go to church, which was about a mile away, she used her bike. When there were night meetings some of the young people who lived in the area accompanied her home as they rode their bikes with her.

The house in which they were meeting was not large enough for growth so the leaders of the church saved money to buy a building. They found a house near Pasar Baru that would be a good place for a church. This was a big house with a little house along side of it for servants or whatever use was practical.

Pastor Loong was not only the editor of a magazine that went to many Chinese speaking people but he was also an outstanding Chinese artist. Some of his paintings sold for unheard-of prices. He also wrote lovely Chinese characters. He taught his boys to write nice Chinese characters as well.

Pastor Loong (on left) the famed artist

The church suggested Pastor Loong take a vacation in the hills where it was cooler and enjoy painting in liesure. These works of art could be sold to make up the needed money for the house for the church. He quite willingly did just that.

The day arrived when he was to have the art exhibit. There were many lovely pieces of animals and landscapes. There were also Chinese Characters on scrolls giving the message of the gospel. Whole verses were written out in his lovely characters. People were proud of his work and sent many lovely flower arrangements thanking him for such an exhibit. Helen Jean was helping Pastor Loong when a guest would come with flowers. As the flowers came she would try to match them with some of the paintings. Wah! That was decidedly the wrong thing to do. Then it looked like a flower exhibit not an art exhibit. Pastor Loong put all the flowers out in the front yard. Helen Jean thought this was a shame because it was so hot out there. Everyday she would take a pile of dead flowers to the garbage. Nevertheless enough of the paintings were sold to pay for the big building but not the small one.

Helen Jean the floral manager

Dr. and Mrs. Low said they would rent the little house. The church wanted to get into the building so took up their offer. Little did they know the Low's future plans nor the trouble they would make for the church.

The big building had many rooms. If the church would tear out the division in the front they could seat about two hundred people. Along the side were more rooms. Pastor could use the room where there was a telephone for his study. It had an outside door. This would be good for any visitors during the day. In the back was a large living room. Between the office and big living room along the side were rooms for bedrooms for the family. Only the office and living room in the back opened to the place for the church.

After the Loong family moved to the church property Helen Jean moved into Pastor Loongs's old home. There was a front yard with a roof where he kept his car but Helen Jean had no car. She had other plans.

When a little girl would see her on the street she would ask her when she would start Sunday School there. So on July 10th the class began in the front yard. Mr. Lee was willing to help Helen Jean but later was very busy so Chen Mu Lin took over. The Lord enabled the group to grow to about two hundred children.

People back home sent Christmas cards, which were given to the children for memorizing their verses. When these home folks get to glory they will get their reward for the numbers who came and really trusted the Lord.

One of Pastor Loong's art panels

Chapter 32
The Lord Increases the Sunday School

The first year Helen Jean was in Indonesia the Lord used her and some of the men of the church to start a Sunday school of 67 children. The men enjoyed using the many helps Helen Jean had brought from America.

While in America Helen Jean had spoken to a group of ladies in Colorado. They asked her if there was anything they could do to help her. These dear ladies had very little money so she suggested a magazine subscription—a Christian one that would challenge her on the field. As soon as she had sent them her address they ordered the magazine. The magazine, in its first issue, advertised a world wide Sunday school Contest. Helen Jean went to Pastor Loong and suggested they enter the contest. He was not interested in it. Helen Jean went back to her house claiming Jeremiah 33:3. For a whole month she prayed that they could enter the contest and that Pastor Loong would be willing to do so.

Another issue came. This time it advertised that the prize for the winning Sunday school would be a lovely bus. Helen Jean took the magazine to Pastor Loong and showed him the picture of the prize. If they were the winners they could really use that bus! As he was looking and reading about the contest he said to Helen Jean, "Let me handle this!" And he did. He called the church together and announced a special Sunday afternoon communion service. This was during the time when most people rested from the heat in Indonesia. About 15 people arrived. Pastor Loong spoke a few words before serving the communion. He made it clear that he had noticed most of the people of the church, including himself, didn't care too much about the souls of children. Many were going to hell and this church was letting them. If anyone wanted to confess their sin before communion do so now. Wah! One after another stood and wept as they did so. What a service! After communion was served Pastor Loong laid plans for the up-coming Sunday school Contest. All 15 people were expected to go calling as many times during the week as possible. Each Friday or Saturday they would meet for six weeks to report how many people they thought from their calling were coming that week. This would help Helen Jean to prepare for the crowd coming.

The week before the contest started when the count was taken for possible people attending there were over 200! When Helen Jean heard this she informed Pastor Loong they needed more chairs. Mr. Yuang said he could donate 50 chairs which were like little stools made from bamboo. With the benches Helen Jean used for her Children's Sunday school in her carport they may be enough.

There was no such thing as a water fountain but children would also want a drink of water before the Sunday school was over. Mrs. Loong said she would boil water for them but needed some large water pots. Others had pots and delivered them to the church. Mrs. Loong boiled water on Saturday so the water would be cool by Sunday.

Wei Nai, Pastor Loong's son, said he would run off Sunday school papers and cut the Chinese stencils. Helen Jean would cut the stencils for the Indonesian Sunday school students.

If over 200 came where should they have classes? From the looks of the lists, children from the primary age would be the largest class unless the Junior Indonesian class was larger.

Daily Choices for Christ

Wei Nai Loong and family
later missionaries in the Philippines,
one daughter a missionary in Russia

If they had rain all would get wet. If they had sun all would be too warm. The suggestion came to put a tent over the back yard and the front yard. Pastor Loong had only one tent. He did have a friend who had a tent so he was elected to go see if they could use it for six weeks. He came back with the tent.

The first Sunday of the contest arrived. The weather was nice—no rain and a bit cloudy. It wasn't too hot and not too cold. The people started to come. Some spoke Indonesian, Mandarin, Keh hwa, and Cantonese. The back yard had a large group of primary children. The front yard had had a good group of Indonesians. When the count was taken there were 289.

When the 15 Faithful met they said they were sure they won the contest. Pastor Loong encouraged them not to be so proud but go calling everyday and bring in 100 more next Sunday.

Helen Jean knew her work was to see that everyone had a chair and a Sunday school paper. Mrs. Loong would take care of the water. Figures for the flannel graph and songs must be made ready by next week.

Mrs. Loong boils drinking water.

The next meeting of the faithful 15 revealed maybe over 400 people would arrive the next Sunday. Where would they seat them? One of the 15 suggested they buy boards to string from one stool to the other. This would be another expense but people promised to pay for enough boards so 400 people could sit. When they set these up most of the boards were in the front yard. The second Sunday 405 children and young people arrived. Very few adults came. Their class was the smallest class we had.

When the 15 met again they praised the Lord for the number who came and that the Gospel was going out. Pastor Loong again challenged the 15 to get 100 more people the third Sunday. That would mean going to new areas of the city to invite people to come. If 100 more were coming Wei Nai and Helen Jean had work to do cutting stencils and running papers for you could not buy Sunday school materials in Djakarta. Some could be ordered from Hong Kong but it would take a month to receive them and they needed papers now.

The third Sunday arrived. Again there was no rain and the weather was a bit cloudy and cool. When the count was taken they had 509 people in the Sunday school.

The 15 were getting tired of calling so often. They complained to Pastor Loong. He told them they were in a contest and wanted to see 600 next Sunday. During this week Pastor Loong was in an accident with his car so he could not use it for a few days.

The fourth Sunday arrived. Again there was no rain and it was a bit cloudy and cool. When the count was taken there were 593 people present.

At the meeting with the 15 he scolded them. The church missed their goal. Now this week they must work harder and get 100 more. That they did. When the count was taken for the 5th week 792 people came. Wah! The back yard was almost full and the front yard was filling up. The church had classes and they too were being filled.

E.G. provides 'air conditioning'

They had one more Sunday before the end of the contest. Pastor Loong met with the 15 faithful and challenged them to go every day and call on people, pray and give. Most of the faithful 15 had given about as much as they could give. They were challenged to give so they could hire trucks to bring in people from areas where there were large numbers coming.

If they would have 1500 people they would need more space for the 5 classes. A suggestion came to get another tent and ask the rice sellers next door if they could use their yard for a few hours on Sunday. No one wanted to ask a businessman for his yard so they voted that Pastor Loong go see about it. He came back saying the people had been wondering what was happening at the church. They were glad for us to use the yard. Pastor Loong also was able to borrow a tent for the yard. Helen Jean informed them they needed chairs again. Everyone was lacking money but Mrs. Lee got up and said, "All of us have beds. Each bed has a number of bed boards or slats. Couldn't we string the slats between the rest of the stools that have no boards?" One of the servants went from house to house and obtained enough bed slats to seat about 1500 people.

Water was a problem. Mrs. Loong needed more huge jars. She boiled 60 gallons of water the day before the last day of the contest. Mrs. Sim, a wealthy lady, saw the walk and kitchen filled with jars and asked what was this? She donated a mix, something like Kool-Aid, to be put in the water for the children.

Wei Nai, the son of Pastor Loong, was about 12 years old and worked most of Saturday on the copier running sheets for the contest. He ran off Sunday school papers, tracts and song sheets in Indonesian and Chinese Characters. There were 14 stencils cut and he ran off 4,112 copies on the copier.

Wei Nai Loong ran the mimeograph
at age 12.

Pastor Loong wanted a picture of the last day of the people who came. The group decided the picture should be taken before the Sunday school started. The man who took the picture brought risers and put them on the sidewalk in front of the church. When people came he had them sit. Four truckloads of people came, cars came, *bedjas* came and people walked. Some were late and missed out in having their picture taken. Helen Jean has a copy of the picture that was taken at that time in her home. When the count was taken there were 1,426 present the last day of the contest. There were 5 teachers and many adults keeping people quiet so they could listen.

The Faithful 15 met and decided they must have seven Sunday Schools, not one big one. Several became the teachers. The smallest Sunday school was about 20 and the largest was a few hundred. Helen Jean was given zipper bags to hold figures, songs, verses and other tools for the Sunday schools. These went out each week to the teachers in their areas.

Once a quarter the students who learned all the verses came to the church for a contest. There were about 400 who came. A story or challenge was always given besides singing. The contest was like a spelling bee in saying the verses, to see who would last the longest.

Helen Jean's vision was to see six more churches started as a result of the Sunday Schools but because of much political opposition she did not see it in her day there. These six Sunday Schools were held in strange places. One was on a large porch of a home. Another in a carport, another in a tearoom which belonged to a man who became a Christian after Pastor Loong dealt with him. He had used his tearoom in the past as an opium den. Another Sunday school was held by a young person who was a Christian. Her mother was also a Christian but her dad was a professional gambler and used his home a gambling den. Another was held in a building used as a church at times. One was held in a Chinese home.

The seventh Sunday school was held in the new church building which had just been purchased where they came for the contest.

Although we didn't come in first over all in the contest and win the bus, we were first in our division and received folding tables, chairs and Sunday school materials. However, no other Sunday school profited as greatly as ours did.

Chapter 33
Result of Visitation

No one was given a crash course in visitation during the Sunday school contest. People just had a burden for people to come and a love for them to come to know their Lord. The men of the church and Pastor Loong had always visited men who needed the Lord. However, after the Sunday school contest, the ladies made it a point to call once a month.

Once a week Helen Jean headed up the calling program of the Young People. The rule was "If you go calling you must be present at the next young People's meeting. The person who called on him or her should welcome them if they came and introduce them to the rest of the young people one by one. If the caller was absent that was a poor testimony."

Most of the young people had bikes. On Sunday afternoons often a gang would go calling together on friends they knew who lived close by. To see six or seven bikes stopping at your house was impressive. One of the young people drove an Austin like a public bus. Often if there were seven who went calling on people who lived a distance from the church, they would use the Austin. He had a certain route and would be back later to pick them up to go elsewhere. When six or seven young people who were dressed properly would arrive at a home, the parents would take note. This club or meeting just might help their child.

Youth out calling on bicycles

One old man did not want his girls to attend our young peoples. The group decided to visit the home. They found the old man sick in bed. Helen Jean suggested the group go in and pray one by one for him. Each of them stood around his bed and offered prayers for his health. The next time they had Young Peoples the girls whose father was sick were present. The young people were Christians so asked about the father. "Oh", they said, "When the group left he felt so good he knew God had answered the young people's prayer." So when his daughters asked if they could attend the Young Peoples meeting he was willing they should go.

During the Sunday school contest Mr. Lee, a leader in the church, and his son went calling. His son was in Primary school, being about nine years old. While dad was talking to the adults or young people he was playing with the children telling them to come to Sunday school. He evidently made it very interesting for him and his dad, since they as a team were the outstanding callers of the Sunday school contest. Mr. Lee was a businessman and had many contacts but his little son challenged more people to come than his dad.

Helen Jean found it was necessary to go calling with a group of both girls and fellows from the Young Peoples because the results were better with a mixed group.

Almost all the young people had friends that they wanted to see become Christians and to be a part of the Young Peoples. Many were friends in school. When the parents found that this was a Chinese Young People's group they were more willing to let their girls come.

The Young People's meeting was done only in Mandarin Chinese. If they attended a Chinese school they could understand the language. This also pleased the Chinese parents. Only the Sunday schools were done in Indonesian.

Tjin Chen & family
Choir director and future deacon

One day Mrs. Loong asked Helen Jean to go calling with her. She knew of a lady who needed some motherly love. When they arrived at the home she invited them to come in to see her baby. The cute little thing was wide-awake. Mrs. Loong prayed with her and they left. A few days later Mrs. Loong told Helen Jean this lady wanted to give away her baby. Mrs. Loong had five children – four boys and one girl – but she did not want another. Mrs. Loong asked Helen Jean if she would like to start an orphanage. Helen Jean made it very clear that was not her calling. She enjoyed the Young Peoples' work and had a hard time enjoying work with the ladies who had all kinds of ideas for Helen Jean's work.

One of the hard things Helen Jean had to do when calling was to drink tea. The first thing given you when you went calling was a glass of hot tea. At first she would ask for water. However she found this was a lot of trouble for some homes so she tried to learn to like tea. Often the tea was made in the morning and put into thermos bottles for visitors or themselves for the day. Water would mean boiling some which would be wasted time. Helen Jean's teeth turned dark from drinking tea. When she went to the dentists at home they asked her if she smoked. Wah! You can't win when you drink tea.

Swei Loong, the president of the Young Peoples, asked Helen Jean to go see his sick younger brother. She expected to see a boy smaller than Swei Loong. When she arrived at the hospital-like place she found a big tall lanky fellow. She immediately coveted him for the Young People's group. After praying for him she suggested that when he was well he should come to Young Peoples. Praise the Lord he did come! He became one of the leaders in the Young People's group and later was the president.

Calling paid off but none of us were experts at it. When Helen Jean came back to America and wanted to go calling in the church she was told she didn't know how to call. She realized two or three of the ladies did all the calling for that church. This made her understand she was taking away their ministry and so she ceased from calling in that church so would be encouraged to continue doing well on their own initiative.

Chapter 34
Young People's Choir

Soon after the church met in the new building, Pastor Loong invited a choir of young people to sing once a month in the church. They were young people from a number of places.

Helen Jean told the young people of the church that they should have their own young people's choir. At that time there were only about fifteen in the young people's group. Most of the young people could read music and knew how to use the do, re, mis. They lacked altos and tenors but Helen Jean filled in for some. All those who sang in the church's young people's choir were Christians. Some were not members yet.

One day Swei Loong brought a schoolmate of his to church. Helen Jean heard his lovely tenor voice and coveted it for the choir, but found that the boy worshipped idols. In his home they had a kitchen god and a glass on the outside door of the house. This glass was to frighten the demons away.

He came to young people's meetings and became a Christian. He then was invited to sing in the choir. His name was E.G.. After he became a Christian he wanted a Christian name. Helen Jean read from her dictionary a list of Christian names for men. When they were almost through the list, he suggested "William". As a result he became known as William Lee.

Pastor Loong doubted that the man was truly saved. He thought he was just saying he was a Christian to be able to sing in the choir.

Pastor Loong asked William if he were a Christian when he wanted to be baptized. He told him he had become a Christian in young people's meeting.

Pastor Loong asked him many questions and William gave all the right answers. But Pastor Loong was still not satisfied so he asked William if he believed the Bible. He said he did.

The next question Pastor Loong asked was, "What do you believe about idols?" William had his Bible with him. He started to look through the New Testament. He told Pastor it was the last verse of one of the books. After some time he found I John 5:21, "Little children keep yourselves from idols." Pastor no longer doubted him. Pastor was pleased that he wanted to be baptized and live according to the Bible. Later, William went to Bible School and still later became a pastor.

E.G. (on left) finally convinced
Pastor Loong that he was a believer.

The young people wanted robes for their choir. Some of the girls sewed for a living. They were willing to sew them. The robes were white with a wide yoke about the neck. They had big sleeves. The body of the robe was shirred onto the yoke. Helen Jean's was the largest.

The choir grew to be about 35 to 40 young people who sang three Sundays each month if the invited choir was not there.

Because there were not enough robes, the young people decided to have new robes. Helen Jean told the young people the church could not afford to provide them, so they would have to pay for their own robes. They readily agreed.

Each person would raise enough money to pay for their own robe, if they could. Shortly after this in the young people's meeting, Helen Jean noticed that a group of young people was talking in low tones. If she came near them they scattered. She knew something was not according as it should be. Whatever it was some were for it, others were not.

From what she could piece together they could buy a ticket and if they won and got the jackpot, that person would pay for the robes.

Immediately, Helen Jean said, "The Lord cannot bless you when you sing in robes produced by gambling." She made it clear that God was the giver, not some gambler.

This did not make Helen Jean very popular but the young people realized they were wrong. Praise the Lord, not long after this, money came for the robes and they were not bought with gambling money.

The choir was invited to sing in different places. The girls wore white gowns with a pink bow from the collar. The young fellows wore white pants and shirts. They wanted ties but to find a number alike was almost impossible. Helen Jean had a sewing machine and soon had pink ties for all the fellows.

Because there were good singers who read do, re, mis in each of the parts, the choir grew. Sunday mornings when the choir sang they often noticed people crying. They were touched by the Lord.

When Helen Jean was in high school she sang in Handel's "Messiah". It was done each year around Christmas time. When a group of singers came from Bandung, a city near Djakarta, they sang part of the "Messiah".

Some of the young people asked if they could learn the "Messiah". Helen Jean suggested they learn about six or seven numbers with the choir and have at least five solos. She had the entire "Messiah" done in notes rather than numbers.

The young people could not learn the English quickly nor could many people understand English. Pastor Chou was willing to translate the English and write the numbers for each part. This was a huge task. He was a friend of those from Bandung so asked for the copy of the song they had sung.

They had done the hard work of translating and changing the notes to numbers of some of the "Messiah" that they would sing in Chinese. Hymnbooks often have no notes on the staff but have numbers representing the notes. One equals do, two re, three mi and so on.

Daily Choices for Christ

Chinese hymnal with numbers for notes

Before the Chinese learn the words they learn the tune by the numbers. This was July so by Christmas they should be able to sing most of the Christmas parts. However, they ended up by singing more than they first thought they could. "Glory to God" was the first completed in numbers and run off on the copier.

When the Indonesian calendar turned red that meant all businesses would be closed for a holiday. When such a day occurred, Helen Jean and the young people went on a picnic. She announced, however, that they would have a choir practice instead this time.

She had helped the director to learn to direct but he seemed not too excited. He and some of the choir members had planned to go to another island. They went, but about 30 of the choir came for practice. Helen Jean had to direct the choir herself. They struggled through each page and learned to sing the do, re, mis of the one whole chorus. They had really made progress! The young people were so encouraged and excited that they could hardly wait for the next practice.

The gang who went for a joy ride in the boat met with a terrible wind. The little boat almost tipped the gang into the ocean. They prayed if they could get back safely they would really work on the "Messiah" and they did. The next practice was really an exciting one.

Christmas night the church was packed. The girls were dressed in white Chinese gowns and the fellows wore white shirts and white pants.

Only the Lord could do a work as He did through those young people. Two of the girls in the group learned to play all the music. This was no little task. The young people worked like beavers, which was unreal, to learn the solos and chorus in such a short time.

The Lord caused the people to come to hear the young people sing. He sang through them in such a way many were challenged. The young people could only give God the glory for the outcome for none were trained singers. The young people ranged from fourteen years old to early twenties. None were married. To hear them pray before they sang was a real delight. Many of them came from poor homes. However, there were a few from homes of wealth.

After working so long on the "Messiah" the young people wanted another song which they could sing. ""Elijah" by Mendelssohn was chosen. They asked the pastor to read the Scripture between singing.

They wanted to act as they sang. The girls decided to wear botic skirts and have a big botic shawl that would cover their head.

Helen Jean sings "Elijah" with Indonesians.

When Elijah prayed, one of the boys acted the part. He insisted they must rig up something so fire would fall. He cut up red paper and tied it to a string pulley. One of the boys in the back let the paper fall just at the right time. The paper was hidden behind the overhang of the platform so people did not see it until it fell. The string was which held the paper not noticeable.

The music seemed much harder for them but they enjoyed doing it for there was a lot of action and Scripture read in Chinese.

Today if you would visit the church you might see one of several choirs singing for a service.

Chapter 35
Yearly Camping

Each year the young people looked forward in going to the other side of Java to the Bible School for a week's outing.

In order to get there they had to take a train to Surabaja then obtain a truck to take them to the Bible School in Malang. Generally Helen Jean would go to the train master and buy all the tickets at once. She would not give the extra money under the table for the train car. Sometimes they needed more than one train car but she was not happy to do this for she could not manage two cars from foolishness. Often when other churches knew they were going they wanted their young people to go with them. This saved their leaders a big headache in getting a train car. Helen Jean made it known if they were going with the Wei Dau Tang young people the outsiders were under the same rules as Wei Dau Tang were. If possible the outsiders were put in the second car and Wei Dau Tang young people were in another.

They would leave Djakarta on the train in the morning and arrive in the evening in Malang. Dinners were expensive so food was brought along. They liked to eat all day long!

One time Helen Jean failed to get two train cars. E.G., the president of the Young Peoples, was not in the car so she asked someone to find him. He came to her and she asked him, "How is your seat?"

"Oh," he said, "I have a high seat."

Later she found he had been standing up most of the way. She immediately made room some way so he could sit down.

Another time she went to the second car and found the young people who said they would follow Wei Dau Tang Young People's rules but were smoking. They had lied about going to camp and they did not intend to come back with the gang nor intend to go to camp.

Indonesia is very warm. During a long train ride often the young people would take off their shoes. Helen Jean also at times felt more comfortable with her shoes off. Often the president of the Young People would sit beside Helen Jean and discuss plans. The president was a young man who really loved the Lord. His responsibility on the trip was to keep the boys in line. Helen Jean took care of the girls. However, if he had difficulties he would share them with Helen Jean. They knew then they had to shape up if they ever expected to go to camp again.

When the president left his seat immediately others would fill it to sit with Helen Jean. Helen Jean was sitting with her shoes off and along came Sin Han. He wanted to sit beside her. He talked to her and then slipped his foot in her shoe. Wah! It just fit. Off he walked.

Immediately Helen Jean shouted, "You have my shoe."

"Oh, so sorry," he said. However he was not sorry one bit. He had motive in his actions. Helen Jean would not know until later why he walked off with her shoe.

Later, July 14th was her birthday. The Young People wanted to give Helen Jean something she would really like. Sin Han said, "I know the perfect gift. A pair of nice comfortable shoes she can wear on Sundays." How could they get a pair of shoes so she wouldn't know about it that would fit? Sin Han assured them he knew her size but it was up to the girls to pick out the right style.

Off they went to the shoe shop. Sin Han sat in the chair for fitting and the girls choose the style.

Indonesians had smaller feet than Helen Jean so they went from shop to shop. Every shop had to know why a fellow would be trying on ladies shoes and none seem to fit. After some time one of the young people suggested they go to a shop where the owners were Christians. The girls were pleased with the styles but Sin Han walked around in one after another of them to see if they were comfortable.

Daily Choices for Christ

At last they found a pair that were cute and passed the comfortable test with Sin Han. They pooled their money but still did not have enough but the owner of the shop was willing to sell them for the money they had since it was going to Helen Jean.

What a surprise Helen Jean received when she opened the box of shoes. How did they buy such comfortable, stylish shoes? They must have cost a mint! Then the young people tried all at once to tell her how they bought them. Helen Jean then said to Sin Han, "You were not sorry one bit that you ran off with my shoe on the train!" He just laughed!

On the train all day with young people helped Helen Jean to know the many troubles that surrounded them at home. The young fellows who came along to help with the luggage often were not Christians but went home different than when they first came.

After camp, often as a result of camp, Wei Dau Tang Church would have opportunity for the young people to be baptized. They would have to go before the church officers to be reviewed before they were presented to the church. Some were rejected but the church accepted most of them.

As a result the Young People's meetings grew and the Sunday morning Young People's Choir increased in number.

Indonesian youth at camp
at the Bible school in Malang

Chapter 36
Home On Furlough

Shortly after the church moved to the new building in Djakarta, Helen Jean went home for her first furlough from the Indonesian work.

She had written her mother she would be home in July and hoped to go to the Baptist Mid-Missions conference. She was given time to speak at the conference which was held in Dr. Robert Gilbert's church. Her Mother found a lovely cotton pink dress which she thought would fit and it did. Helen Jean was so happy for it. She had white gloves but needed a hat.

When she arrived at the conference Helen Jean asked if they had any hats in the missionary cupboard. There were none that would go with her pink dress. Mrs. Cook, missionary from Peru, and Helen Jean took off to buy a hat. They found a white and pink one that would go well with the dress. She had washed her white gloves and starched them so they almost looked like leather. She was ready to speak as far as clothes were concerned, she thought.

When she came back from the store with Mrs. Cook, supper was being served. As they lined up, someone with a big voice made a remark about the lady with the pink and white hat. When Helen Jean was introduced before speaking, Dr. Gilbert called her 'Cover Girl'.

Poor Helen Jean was so embarrassed but when she came into the church auditorium she noticed the Baptist Mid-Missions' magazine. On the front cover was a picture of a group of the young people, deacons, Pastor Loong and Helen Jean. This picture was taken when the new building was dedicated in Indonesia.

When Helen Jean got up to speak, she was so embarrassed but had to say something. She said, "I am a 'cover girl', look at the cover of the Baptist Mid-Missions' magazine you have in the rear of the church.

The Lord spoke through her and afterwards Pastor Gilbert would not let the hat rest. He told the church how Helen had wanted a hat from the cupboard but had to buy one. Now he was suggesting if anyone would like to help Helen pay for her hat the line forms in front of her! The people lined up and some gave one or two dollars or change. Helen Jean received enough money to pay for the hat.

From this event Helen Jean learned that ladies had ceased to wear hats to church. It isn't so funny how things change so quickly when you are out of the U. S. Every time she came home she had to be observant what ladies did and wore.

Almost every time Helen Jean came home, she had a debt in the home office for her plane or ship ticket. This meant she would have to save every bit she could to get this paid and save enough to go back in a year. She felt led to speak at camps in the summer in spite of the fact she was not given much to pay off her debt or to help her go again. However, the Lord knew he wanted to use her at camp and always supplied the needed funds when she was ready to go.

Because her parents were interested in her staying home and teaching school she managed to take meetings back to back before she went back to the field, weary but happy.

There were times between meetings she was so weary she would go to a quiet hotel to sleep and get her clothes washed and ironed for the next meetings. Sometimes her two brothers' and sister's homes were a haven of rest because they were near the next meetings. Not often did she have the opportunity to stay in one place for a week except at a campsite.

Her brother gave her a big white piece of luggage. She was so happy for this for it held most of her things. As a result she had only one piece of luggage to check. Her sister had given her a white small case for carry-on luggage.

Almost all her traveling was done by Greyhound bus for she had no car. The Greyhound bus offered clergy rates to missionaries. By using this she was able to save a good sum.

Helen Jean chose to sit in the front of the bus. When the door was opened, she would get some fresh air. Many people smoked on the bus and when you would arrive, your clothes smelled like tobacco. Helen Jean called it "Bus Cologne."

Helen Jean never wore the clothes she wore on the bus when she would speak in a service. She just did not want to smell like the bus. Sometimes she would arrive at the church just in time to change clothes in their restroom and wash up.

As she traveled Helen Jean needed to carry her slide projector and slides of the field onto the bus. She praised the Lord that with all the traveling she did, her projector still worked.

Chapter 37
Be Of Good Courage

Chen Mu Lin was one of the faithful deacons who loved the Lord. He wanted to see people come to know the Lord Jesus personally. His wife was an Indonesian and so did not come to the Chinese services.

On December 5, 1957, Mr. Chen's baby died. Many Indonesians wrapped their dead babies in a mat and put them in the garbage. Chen Mu Lin did not want to do this. He had taken his baby to the hospital for treatment but it died. He asked pastors to perform a funeral for the baby. They could not be bothered. In desperation he asked Helen Jean to help him. She went to the hospital and dressed the baby in a nice little gown. The mother was too sick to do this. Chen Mu Lin had obtained a tiny coffin and bought a place in the cemetery to bury it. When Helen Jean was fixing the baby it moved. Was the baby really dead? According to the doctor the baby was dead.

The weather was not helpful for a funeral because it was raining. Nevertheless, in the rain, Helen Jean and Chen Mu Lin sang "Jesus Loves Me". After this, Helen Jean spoke a few words and prayed. The casket was lowered into the grave. Dirt went down upon the casket and the grave was filled. There were no flowers piled on the grave just raindrops to settle the grave.

Some of the deacons were not as faithful to the Lord as Chen Mu Lin. Mr. Syeh wanted his daughter to have a Chinese education. He found a school that he thought had a high standard of education but was run by the Communists.

Gwo Yin, his daughter, was a Christian so he thought she could study there and not become a Communist. When Helen Jean came back from furlough she found Gwo Yin was taking charge of the Young People and had a Sunday school class.

The first Sunday Helen Jean walked through the Sunday school to see who was teaching and how. The primary children were meeting in the back of the church. She went there and found Gwo Yin teaching them a Communist song. On the spot, she stopped the song and told Gwo Yin she could not teach Sunday school. This did not make Helen Jean too popular. She found another teacher to teach the Bible in Sunday school.

Helen Jean took over the Young Peoples again and found some of the deacons were in favor of their children going back to red China to be educated after high school.

Upon further investigation she found that other Chinese churches in Djakarta had lost most of their young people because they went back to red China for their education after high school.

In May, Shyu Yan dropped out of Young Peoples. May 17 Helen Jean learned she had gone back to China for her education. From then on if young people were missing in the Young People's meeting, the young people and Helen Jean would go visit them. If they saw piles of boxes and things ready for shipping, Helen Jean and the gang would pray that something would happen so they could not go. As a result they had only three who went from their group while Helen Jean was there.

Another event that happened to help the young people from going to China was the news which came back from Da Tung's brother. He was having one terrible time in China.

Every one who came to Young Peoples at that time knew the Lord. Praying was just part of the service. You could call on anyone to pray. This was one way the Communists could not influence them. If we asked someone to pray and they were a Communist, they would just leave.

On June 20, Helen Jean asked Deacon Yaung if he was a Communist. His answer was that he was a Christian Communist.

Mr. & Mrs. Geh loved the Lord and gave their lives for full time service. She was a hairdresser. She ran a shop that became popular among the ladies. She put her husband through Bible school with funds from her shop. He went to Hong Kong for his training. When he finished he was an evangelist. He and his wife sang nicely together so she helped him then in his ministry. They had two children. They held meetings on some of the other islands of Indonesia with good results.

Mr. and Mrs. Geh dedicated to the ministry

Mr. Lyou was a teacher who loved the Lord. He contracted tuberculosis. He told the Lord if He would heal him, he would give his life for full time service. The Lord did just that but he went back to teaching. Very shortly after teaching a few days he started to bleed and died. God took him. His death really challenged people to keep their word with the Lord.

On September 9, 1960, at eleven o'clock p.m., there was a rattle at the gate. Pyau Ron, sister of Sin Han, came for help. She asked

Helen Jean to come to her home to see Sin Han. He had tried to kill himself. Helen Jean quickly dressed and went with Pyau Ron. When they arrived, Pyau Ron took Helen Jean to Sin Han's bedroom. There he lay all dressed up in his Sunday best, necktie and all. Beside him was a note he had written that he had taken nine grams of pentobarbital and wanted to die.

Helen Jean told Pyau Ron that there was still hope, he was still living. If they could get the doctor to pump his stomach he would be all right. He was like a big sack of wheat to get into a *bedja*, to find the doctor who lived behind the church.

When they arrived at the doctor's home, the servants said the doctor had gone to sleep. Helen Jean insisted he get up immediately and help them. The doctor was not too happy to get up but he did, and pumped his stomach. Most of the medicine came up but he was still trying to sleep. The doctor could not waste anymore time on him. He told Helen Jean to wake him up every fifteen minutes if he slept. After three o'clock he should be ok. It was now one o'clock. He was taken to the church's guest bedroom and Helen Jean went in every fifteen minutes to wake him up. By three o'clock he was really fussing to be awake. They knew he was getting better. Swei Sz, the servant, came to relieve Helen Jean. By morning, Swei Sz announced that Sin Han was crabby and ok.

On September 11 they had to take him to a mental ward. There they were able to help him get over wanting to kill himself for the time being. Helen Jean told the American consulate's doctor, Dr. Slocum, about Sin Han. Dr. Slocum was a son of missionaries under Baptist Mid-Missions. They had served in Africa. Dr. Slocum wanted to see and talk to him. Helen Jean arranged for them to meet in her study in the evening, which was a good time for each of them.

Dr. Slocum found out Sin Han had more than one problem. Mainly he wanted to marry a girl they knew but her father would not give permission. The father, no doubt, knew more about his conduct than any of them did. Dr. Slocum spoke to him very forcefully and from then on he ceased to come on a regular basis to Young Peoples. Whenever he needed help, however, he came to Helen Jean's study for counsel.

Before Helen Jean came back from furlough, her brother gave her a lovely wall clock. She hung it in her study. Everyone who saw it admired it. Once day the Lord dealt with Helen Jean to give her clock away to the person who would learn the most Scripture before her next furlough.

She listed verses to learn and then books to memorize. Every verse had to be said word perfect. This would help them spiritually when unbelievers would cause them trouble.

Pan Wan Young was a married lady who oversaw sewers who made clothing. She sat at a desk, inspecting sewing, giving out needed supplies and helped where they were having trouble. Often she was just waiting. During those times she learned scripture. When she came to say verses she would say one or two chapters word perfect. Her desire was to learn the entire New Testament. Some of the older ladies who came to the Ladies Meeting also learned verses.

Helen Jean was given a big box of buttons, so she gave them a button for every verse. Some of the ladies made clothes for their husbands and would take shirt buttons, all alike. They had to learn eight to nine verses in order to get the same kind of button.

The young people also learned verses as well as the children. Scripture learning really helped many turn from sin and turn from Communism. All wanted the clock but Pan Wan Young managed to be the winner.

Chapter 38
Alone on the Station

After Pastor Loong and his family left for Hong Kong Helen Jean was left alone with the work in Djakarta. The church hired four different pastors. The first was an elderly Chinese man who was there until another pastor could be found. Rev. Chen, a good Bible teacher, and his family came and he was used to help the church grow. He and his wife loved the Lord and did a good work. However, he found it difficult to work with some of the deacons who called themselves Christian Communists.

One day Helen Jean happened to be at the church just as Rev. Chen and his family were eating. She noticed how little was on the table. As soon as she could she invited the deacons and pastor over for tea. They all came wondering what was going to happen. They discussed church affairs and then Helen Jean asked them to raise the pastor's salary for they did not have enough to eat. Her words were like a bombshell. The deacon who lived next door invited the other deacons to come to his house. The pastor and Helen Jean were left to pray. Praise the Lord! He answered prayer and the pastor's family received the benefit.

Sometime later Rev. Chen received a call from the Philippine Islands to teach in a Bible School. This was his first love so we lost our good pastor. When the family left a new pastor was found.

It was time for Helen Jean to go on furlough again. While she was home the church took over her house and gave her two rooms in the church when she came back. Her study/living room was on the front of the church and directly behind it was a room she used for her bedroom.

One morning she noticed people coming and going through the church gate. All were ladies who were strangers looking for Mrs. Low who was a ladies' doctor. When Helen Jean had been in America the Lows had made a door from one of the windows to their house, which opened to the church's back yard. The Lows had Mrs. Low's patients come through this door which opened into the church's back yard. They also used the church's back yard to do their laundry even on Sundays. Her husband, also a doctor, had his patients came through the Lows' own yard gate. However, the Lows had rented only the house on the side of the church and the small yard and gate. They had no business using the church's yard or gate.

One morning Helen Jean looked out of her study window and saw an Indonesian flag and a Communist flag over the gate of the church and over the Lows' gate. Immediately Helen Jean put her American flag on her door to her study which could be seen from the street. Again Helen Jean had to have a deacons' meeting. She must warn them of the danger the church was in flying the two flags. Praise the Lord! After the meeting only the Indonesian flag flew over the church's gate. What the Lows did was their business.

The Lows had not rented the yard of the church or the backyard of the church so the door became a window again and the medical laundry was done elsewhere. No longer were Mrs. Low's patients allowed to come through the church.

Swei Sz was hired to keep the church clean. He was a good worker and professed to be a Christian. He was a son of a head-hunter in Borneo but was raised by one of the Christians in Djakarta. He had a hot temper and at times had a hard time controlling it.

Helen Jean and her language teacher were working in the hall where it was cool. They both looked up when Swei Sz came carrying a sack of something. He passed them and went toward the gate. Helen Jean ran after him and asked him what he had. He did not answer her but ran to get on the public Austin taxi. The driver saw the situation and told Swei Sz to answer her. He did not want to, so the driver told him to get off the auto. Swei Sz got off and went over to Helen Jean and banged her on the head with the bag, which was

Daily Choices for Christ

full of rice. He had taken it from the church's storeroom. He then ran to his room in the back of the church.

Helen Jean's teacher was shocked to see the disrespect Swei Sz had for Helen Jean. She told Helen Jean her police son would figure out something to make his thinking change. Later in the day the police came demanding Swei Sz go to the police station. When they arrived at the police station they asked him some questions.

"Did she first hit you?"

Swie Sz answered, "Oh! no, no, she wouldn't do that!"

"Then why did you hit her?" they asked.

He said, "She wanted to know what was in the bag."

"You mean you hit an American because she asked you a question! Take him to a cell and lock him up!"

Helen Jean's teacher told her to go to the police station the next morning and bring him home. You can believe Swei Sz prayed that night! So the next morning Helen Jean went to the police station to see Swei Sz. Helen Jean was right. He had slept very little.

She asked, "Why are you here, Swei Sz?"

He replied, "Because I hit you. I'm so sorry."

"Okay, Swei Sz, let's go home."

They unlocked the cell and Swei Sz and Helen Jean went back to the church. From then on he was a big help to Helen Jean.

The church building was about four or five blocks from the White House used by the Indonesian government. The Communists wanted the church building for their soldiers but Helen Jean, an American, lived there.

The Communistic Christian deacon Yuang had a plan. He would try to get the Young People to help him kidnap Helen Jean and take her to another island so there wouldn't be an American living in the church. One of the young people drove a public taxi. He could be paid to take her to the seaport where a ship would be waiting. Several of the young people would have to go with her because it was supposed to be a Young People's outing that would take place late at night.

When Helen Jean got wind of their plans she knew that something was not right and told Swei Sz not to go to the church gate and let anyone come into the church at night. Since Swei Sz's trip to the police station he did what Helen Jean wanted.

The gang was supposed to come for Helen Jean at 12 o'clock midnight. Helen Jean got on her knees and prayed. Something happened. She had peace and went to bed and slept. The plan to kidnap Helen Jean did not work. They would have to think of some other plan and plan they did. This time they would leave the young people out of their plans for the young people realized Helen Jean had a real love for each of them since they had come to know the Lord.

Chapter 39
Making Room for more Members

When Helen Jean arrived in Indonesia Pastor Loong and about twenty-five believers were meeting in a dinning and living room in the home of a wealthy lady who owned a tin mine in Singapore.

The men realized they needed a building of their own. Of the twenty-five who met with Pastor Loong only two or three were ladies. All the rest were Chinese businessmen. All were looking for a building for the church. They found a house downtown Djakarta about three or four blocks from the White House of the government. The building was also near a popular market place called "Pasar Baru". By pooling all their resources they were able to buy it. This was an unheard of thing in Djakarta for land and buildings are not sold like they are in America.

A group of Indonesian men came and tore out walls to make a large room for the church. Along the side of this large room rooms were left for living quarters for Pastor Loong and family. He had four boys and a baby girl. A large room was left in the back for dinning and sitting rooms. Chairs were brought and placed in the big church room. It would now hold about 200 people.

There was an aisle down the middle of the room and chairs on each side. One side was for the ladies and the other for men. However the men's side filled up first. When the ladies came the children always sat with them so after the Sunday school contest the church needed more room. Again the Indonesian workers were called to rebuild for another building could not be found big enough for their use.

Pastor Loong had gone to Hong Kong with his family to care for the magazine he published each month. The deacons and Helen Jean must manage the rebuilding. Each day one of the group over saw the workers. Helen Jean took her turn as well as the men. Someone had to be on duty to oversee the workers and see that roof tiles, cement and other things were not carried away by the people who thought they needed them worse than the church.

By this time Helen Jean was living in the church. During the day while workers were there all you could see was nothing but dust and dirt. Clothes had to be washed after the workers were gone and taken off the line before they came the next morning. Food had to be prepared and supplies had to be obtained before the time workers arrived the next morning.

An Indonesian wheelbarrow

A platform was made at one end of the building. The baptistery was below this. One day Helen Jean went to look over what yet had to be done and heard a splash! Splash! Swei Sz, the servant, had decided the baptistry was a nice private swimming pool. He soon found out you do not use a baptistry for your private swimming pool.

The Lord used the Chinese businessmen who were believers to pay the bills on the building and running the church. They could not expect any funds from America. It was their church.

During the time of rebuilding the deacons suggested they not have church meetings. People could visit other churches. The Young People need not meet. When Helen Jean heard of their disbanding the church for building purposes she immediately had a deacon's meeting to suggest they borrow another church's building during the building process. Her suggestion went over like a lead balloon but they realized she was right. They borrowed a church for afternoon meetings but wanted the Young Peoples to be stopped completely. Again Helen Jean had to go to bat for the Young Peoples. They met in the hall, which she would prepare each week for their meetings and choir practice. She did not allow them to go into the part of the church building, which was under construction.

The new church filled rapidly
during the Sunday school contest.

No one seemed to know if this reconstruction was a trick to get the church building ready for the red soldiers or not.

When the building was finished they had space for about 400 people. The Young People's choir was singing every Sunday morning. The platform would not hold that many people so Helen Jean suggested they build steps up to the platform where they could stand. The deacons were not happy about this idea so the Young People obtained wooden risers, which would hold about 40 people. These risers were built so they could be put up and taken down quickly. They were in sections so they could be used elsewhere when they were asked to sing outside the church. As a result the Young People were glad for them. The boys enjoyed getting them ready when they sang outside the church.

After the church was rebuilt Helen Jean lived in two rooms in the back of the church. Off the side of the pulpit was her bedroom with her clothes cupboard in front of the door leading to the platform. On the other side was the pastor's study. Helen Jean's study was across the breezeway, which formerly was a servant's room. This was her living space until she left for furlough.

After furlough they needed to rebuild again. This time they needed Sunday school space. They built a two-story building in back. They used all the space they had on their lot to the alley. On the other side of the alley was a lovely home built by a man from India.

The men of the church thought it would be nice to have a third story and a place to sit and cool off in the open air. All went well until someone leaned over the rail and spit. The Indian man thought they had it in for him and made it known he was not happy with their rooftop playhouse. New rules were then enforced.

Since Helen Jean left the station they have rebuilt more than once.

Chapter 40
Anything Could Happen

After the Sunday school rooms were built in the back of the church Helen Jean was given two rooms on the second floor. All these rooms were built off a long hallway like a porch open to the back yard. Steps to the hallway were near the back wall of the property. These rooms were intended in the future to be used by guests of the church who came for special meetings. Each room had a screen on the window and a set of steel bars from top to bottom like a prison to protect the contents of the room. The door had a lock and also a bolt on the inside.

Helen Jean was happy for these two rooms with a bathroom down the hallway of the open porch on the second floor. A suggestion was give her to make her bedroom in the end room but Helen Jean had other ideas. The bathroom would be too far away for it was located almost at the other end of the hall porch. A suggestion was made that she put her bed in the corner of that end room.

Again she thought differently but said nothing. After she got her things on the second floor she decided to make the end room her study. The corner where they suggested she put her bed was dark and away from the window so she put very little there. Helen Jean was happy in her new rooms. Pastor Loong's brother-in-law made her some furniture that pleased her well.

One night when she was in her bedroom working she heard someone on the roof. A man was taking out the window tile and replacing it with ordinary tile. He needed it more, he thought, than

Helen Jean needed it. This made the room much darker but evidently he was told to do the job. Helen Jean did not know but it was done and would not be changed. As soon as she could she reported the event to the deacons. Some were concerned but others just laughed.

When one can not get the situation changed on the mission field you learn to live around it. That was Helen Jean's lot.

Helen Jean was given an electric refrigerator while she was home on furlough. The deacons decided the best place for it was in Helen Jean's rooms. Her study was full so it went into the bedroom. She was also given a big white coffeepot. She took out trays and it fit into the refrigerator.

When Helen Jean had choir practice she would bring her white coffee pot down full of cold water that had been boiled. What a joy it was to the choir members. The refrigerator not only made cold water for the choir but it was a real room cooler if the door of the refrigerator was opened when the heat was unbearable.

Helen Jean was happy in spite of the unrest in the capital city where she lived.

One night she went to bed and was so weary from the mission work she went sound asleep. She did not know how long she slept but heard a terrible noise in her study. The noise sounded like rocks were coming down from the roof. She got her electric lights on and went to see what happened. In the corner where some suggested she put her bed she saw a pile of tile, cement and debris. The Lord spared her life. Had she placed her bed there as suggested, she would have been killed.

The next day was clean up and repair day. Helen Jean praised the Lord for all those who were kind to her.

The church had a high strong iron fence around the front yard. This protected the church from many unwanted visitors. At night in order to get into the property the people would rattle the gate and Swei Sz would go to see what they wanted.

A young pastor who had a church not far away decided to go see Helen Jean. She will never know if he was paid to do this or not. Swei Sz knew him so let him into the property. When he got in he went straight upstairs and walked into Helen Jean's bedroom. She was fully dressed but was shocked he did not knock or call to

Daily Choices for Christ

her. She took one look at him and decided he was not there for a good reason and moved to the door. She opened it and walked onto the open porch. He called to her but she told him to come to the porch. Swei Sz was near below and could help her if she needed help. Helen Jean never did find out why he came or what his intentions were. She informed Swei Sz never to let him in again without watching him.

The deacons decided Helen Jean had had some stressful days and needed vacation. Not far from their Chinese work was a church that worked with the Indonesians and English-speaking people. They needed a speaker for a conference up in the hills where it was cool. This church had a single male missionary. Some ladies came and invited Helen Jean to speak on the traits typical of most children. She told them when she was in seminary she had a book which was in her book box that she could use.

The day soon arrived when the ladies came back in a car to take Helen Jean to the conference. Many of their church people were going to the hills in a bus. The bus started out before the car full of ladies and Helen Jean. When the ladies arrived the bus had not arrived. It had been stopped a few times looking for an American.

Helen Jean was given a room by herself away from the rest and was guarded by those of the church. Helen Jean was told to stay in her room as much as she could. She did not mind for in order to present a good message she needed time to think and pray. Every time she spoke people stood by the windows keeping an eye on the outside as well as trying to get as much of the message as they could.

The week ended and the ladies took Helen Jean back to Djakarta. Again, the bus was searched but never the car in which Helen Jean rode.

Mr. Yuang, the Communistic deacon, was at the church when Helen Jean arrived. He looked up in surprise and said, "Why are you here?"

She said, "This is my home." And went to her rooms. Mr. Yuang went to see Mrs. Low. Both were in favor of the soldiers living in the church. But what to do with Helen Jean? After getting their heads together they felt if she got married she would leave the church and go live with her husband somewhere else. Another thought she might go home.

Immediately Mr. Yuang went to have a conference with Helen Jean. He delivered the ultimatum: either get married or go home. Helen Jean assured him she did not intend to do either unless the Lord so directed her.

"Christian Baptist Church of Djakarta" in 1965

Chapter 41
The Ultimatum – Go Home or Get Married!

The Overseas Fellowship Mission, formerly the China Inland Mission, had a work in Djakarta. They had a staff of workers living in Djakarta at the headquarters for the Mission. One of their missionaries worked in a Chinese Church not too far from Helen Jean's work. Their headquarters missionaries invited Helen Jean to dinner.

At the dinner they told her of the single missionary who had been doing a good work among the young people was sent home because of unpleasant things which happened in the church where she was working. They suggested Helen Jean should go home or she might end up having a bad reputation like this missionary had which was not true. The fact was they didn't know there were Communistic Christians in Wei Dau Tang who already had given Helen Jean a bad name.

Mr. Fetzer, a man of God in the Home Office of Helen Jean's mission, wrote to her. From what the radio and papers were saying no one would blame her if she came home. The question on Helen Jean's mind was, "What does the Lord want me to do?" So far it seemed the Lord wanted her to stay put, and stay put she did.

Mr. Yuang invited Stephen Tong to come to the church for special meetings. He would make Helen Jean a good husband. He and his brothers were good Christians. He was still in Bible School but soon would be graduating. Stephen had special evangelical meetings using the black board and a piece of chalk. He was also a good choir leader so the choir enjoyed his ministry. He also went calling with the young people and Helen Jean. However, to Mr. Yuang's disappointment, he went back to school and was not interested in Helen Jean.

Mrs. Low suggested there were a number of fellows in the Young Peoples who could be interested in Helen Jean. But to her disappointment they either had someone else in mind or they were not interested. It seemed the Lord wanted Helen Jean to remain single!

Because of the political unrest some young people went to Australia, Holland, Hong Kong, or Taiwan—any place that would take them away from the war. E.G. and his fiancée came to see Helen Jean. E.G. said they were also leaving for Hong Kong as soon as they were married. Helen Jean prayed for them. While she was praying for them Swei Sz brought another visitor to see Helen Jean. He stood there and listened as Helen Jean prayed in Chinese and cried with real tears because they had to leave. She said good bye to them and they left.

The new visitor was a relative of Helen Jean's dad. He worked in the American Consulate. He had come to tell her that he was in charge of all the Americans in Djakarta and it was urgent that every American leave before the war took place in Djakarta.

"Oh, I can't leave," she said. "The mission buys my ticket and I have no money to go."

"Not a problem," Dale said. "The American Government will pay your way and bill your mission and you can pay them. The important thing is to get out now. I will get the men to get your luggage and it will go by ship in a container. I will be after you in a *bedja* when I confirm the air tickets."

No one but Swei Sz, E.G. and his future wife knew that Dale had come, nor why he came.

For Helen Jean it was very difficult to leave her work. She loved the people in Indonesia but if it meant death to her how could she work there? If her presence endangered her brothers and sisters in Christ, was that any favor to them? Was this God showing her He had a work somewhere else for her? She believed God could stop

Daily Choices for Christ

the plans for her leaving if that was His will so she packed up things for the plane home.

She decided to take a suitcase full of food so if Dale and she were separated before they arrived at the airport she would have something safe to eat. The airport was a long way from where Helen Jean lived. With soldiers in the street and planes with loud speakers overhead speaking bitter words against Americans, anything could take place. Both Dale and Helen Jean could be killed. However God protected that one lone *bedja* going to the airport so it arrived safely.

Helen Jean immediately boarded the waiting plane but what about Dale? He had to go back to the American Embassy Building that was twice as far as the two of them had already come. But again the Lord protected Dale and later he too arrived safely in the United States. Since she left right away and didn't need all the food she gave it to the three young people who saw her off.

Helen Jean had a fat pad of tickets with arrangements for her to stay in certain hotels, which included transportation to and from the different airports when she arrived and departed on her long trip home to America.

Years ago when her uncle had seen her off from America he had given her two silver dollars. She never spent them. At this time that was all the money she had in hand and she was on her way half way around the world.

After Helen Jean retired at Missionary Acres, she went back to visit Indonesia in. The church had become a mega church. Instead of using Keh Hwa and Gow Yu Chinese now they had added Indonesian and English.

Jin Syan, who was the Young People's choir director while Helen Jean was there, was now chief deacon. Shwen Ngo, who was one of the chief sopranos in the Young People's Choir, now was leader of the ladies' work. Swei Loong, who had been the first young person to give his life for full time service was the Senior Pastor of the church.

Mr. Yuang and Dr. and Mrs. Low had gone on to their reward.

The church had outstations almost as large as Wei Dau Tong was when Helen Jean first came to Indonesia. The visit was a blessing, sort of the icing on the cake. God had been at work through all of the difficulties faced in those wonderful years in Indonesia.

Missionary service is not just a career, but a state of the heart that beats for the Lord of the Harvest. Once the doors of service in Indonesia were closed to Helen Jean she found that other doors of opportunity were standing wide open. She could not cease being a missionary, only one in Indonesia.

She followed invitations in the years that followed to serve in Canada and then out in Hawaii, a bit closer to her beloved Indonesia. Helen Jean then returned to the Home Office of Baptist Mid-Missions to play a vital role in the T.I.M.E. Ministry, or Theological Instruction and Ministry Enrichment. This provided training resources for the hundreds of missionaries who by 1980 served on every continent of the world. She also set up the library in the mission Home Office for both English and foreign books, with a complete card catalog.

In 1986, when "the mission on the move" relocated from downtown Cleveland out in the suburbs closer to the international airport, this "missionary on the move" made her way to Missionary Acres to continue serving the Lord with other retired missionaries. This was certainly not the end of missionary service, only a new venue for service. From there, she was able in 1991 to revisit old friends in Indonesia, now grown up and gone on in serving the Lord. It was a precious capstone to a lifetime of service, like the interest on an investment of life and love.

From her ministry base at Missionary Acres, Helen Jean continued to teach one day a week as a ministry at the Mountain Park Baptist Academy near Patterson, Missouri. She enjoyed teaching bells, piano, organ, and drums, besides giving the students devotions from the Bible in every class she taught.

When a missionary asks, "Was it worth it all?" the answer is always spelled out in the names of all the people who were won to Christ, trained to serve, and encouraged to grow. We draw our satisfaction from the success of our successors. Helen Jean finished up deeply satisfied.

Daily Choices for Christ

Helen Jean Moose around 1985

God Gives Credit to those Deserving It

This book could not be written without a host of people who have helped me, so some acknowledgments are in order.

First, I want to thank God for giving me parents who taught me to work and not be a quitter. I also enjoy this retirement home that they made possible for me to have. It has been a real blessing during the time of writing this book.

I want to thank my two brothers and sister who opened their homes to me while having meetings and the encouragement they gave.

I want to thank my teachers who had patience so I learned to read, write and do many things from first grade through many other schools.

I will ever be grateful to the people who hired me to work for them while attending school so that I could pay my bills.

I must praise the Lord for Baptist Mid-Missions who put up with me and helped me in so many ways. Only heaven will reveal what an impact these godly men and women had on my life.

I praise the Lord for the many families who entertained me in their homes during deputation days.

I cannot forget the many churches that had a part in my support and still do. Nor can I forget the people who gave me gifts for the work on the field.

May I not forget those who had nothing to give but encouraged my soul with their friendliness and kindness.

I have forgotten the name of the child who gave me a dime at camp, but have never forgotten that she wanted me to have it.

I want to thank the churches and pastors who encouraged me.

I also want to thank Mrs. Joan Nichols, Mrs. Dorothy Selden, Mrs. Roberta Brumbaugh and Dr. William Smallman for their hours of hard work on the book..

For all those who prayed for me these many years, I pray God will give you a good reward also.

I give thanks to those who wrote letters while I was alone on the station so may years. This told me I was not just a name but a person they cared about. You too, will have your reward for it cost you time and money to get the letters off.

For the ladies groups who sent packages during those hard years alone may the Lord remember your labor of love. The buttons you sent to challenge the ladies to learn verses were a big help for the ladies' work. The Christmas and greeting cards challenged the children to learn verses and will never be forgotten.

A belated gift from God in His good timing was my dear husband, Rev. Hilbert Zwyghuizen, whom I had met over forty years earlier. He came to Missionary Acres, the retirement center of Baptist Mid-Missions and the Lord led us together. He was so patient to postpone our wedding until the youth choir I was training at Mountain Park Baptist Academy near Patterson, Missouri, could master "The Hallelujah Chorus." Dr. Gerald Webber, president of Continental Baptist Mission with whom Hilbert had served, tied the knot, and the president of our mission, Dr. Gary Anderson, came to give away the bride. Who could have guessed that a couple of old Midwest missionaries could be so happy together? Wah! Old? Well, he was 77 but I was only 76 when we married. We enjoyed nine wonderful years together before the Lord called Hilbert Home.

However, this book could not have been written had it not been for the Lord Jesus Christ who, bled, suffered and died on the cross for my sin. He saved me and called me into His service to work for Him. Without His strength, power, and wisdom continually given to me I would not have been able to do anything for Him. All praise to Him for whatever was done that was worthwhile!

Meet the Author

Helen Jean Moose served as a full-career missionary with Baptist Mid-Missions, an independent Baptist mission agency based in Cleveland, Ohio. She completed 40 years of active missionary service including the years she spent in China and then Indonesia as described in this book. Her ongoing ministry was in partnership with church planters in Hawaii and Alaska. In her latter years Helen Jean served in one of the instructional programs of the mission on behalf of all of the missionaries, by then well over 1000 in about 50 nations of the world. See www.BMM.org to learn more of Baptist Mid-Missions.

Missionary Acres, in Silva, Missouri, is the retirement center of Baptist Mid-Missions, and is the current happy home and ministry base of Helen Jean Moose Zwyghuizen.

LaVergne, TN USA
05 March 2011
218970LV00002B/42/A